THE

Samaritan

PROJECT

ROB A. FRINGER & JEFF K. LANE

the **HOUSE** studio

The House Studio
PO Box 419527
Kansas City, MO 64141

Copyright 2012 by Rob A. Fringer and Jeff K. Lane

ISBN 978-0-8341-2839-2

Printed in the United States of America

Editor: Kristen Allen

Cover Design: J.R. Caines
Interior Design: Sharon Page and J.R. Caines

www.thehousestudio.com

10 9 8 7 6 5 4 3 2 1

Contents

INTRODUCTION   4

1 THE STORY BEGINS   10

2 WHY ASK WHY?   26

3 UNDERSTANDING OURSELVES IN THE STORY   44

4 WHO IS MY NEIGHBOR?   66

5 DEFINING DISTANCE   88

6 MODERN-DAY SAMARITANS   106

7 EXTENDING THE CIRCLE OF CONCERN   132

8 SERVING THE "OTHER"   152

9 CONTINUING THE STORY   170

Introduction

THE STORY ABOUT THE STORY

As you will quickly see, this book flows out of the Parable of the Good Samaritan in Luke 10:25-37. You will also learn that the book is not only about this parable. Really, the parable is a springboard to discuss a variety of subjects that all focus on learning to love well. In learning to love well, we continue our journey of transformation, a journey on which we begin to look more and more like Christ as we partner with others in order to transform the world around us.

NAVIGATING THE NEIGHBORHOOD

Here's what you will find as you read this book:

1. Lots of questions!

We don't know how many questions there are; we lost count. So if your primary reason for reading a book is to get answers to your questions, *The Samaritan Project* may frustrate you. This book isn't about us giving you the "right" answers: even if we knew the answers for our context, they wouldn't necessarily work in yours. Life and faith and relationships are complex and complicated. A book this size (not to mention the authors of this book) couldn't possibly unpack everything we address on these pages.

The Samaritan Project is about entering into a conversation. As you move through the book, you will find that each chapter contains several pause points. It is at these points that you will find questions and projects that will allow you to reflect further on what you have read. They will challenge and stretch you.

At the end of each chapter you will also find a set of questions called Small Group Transformation Questions. These are designed to stimulate small group conversation.

2. Lots of projects!

"You want us to do work?"

Well, yes and no. These projects are not intended to give you busy work or to make you feel like you have accomplished something. The projects are about putting feet to what you are reading. They are a way to go deeper. They are a way to continue the conversation.

CHOOSING YOUR PATH ON THE JOURNEY

Since this isn't a typical book, we wanted to give you a few options as to how you may best utilize it for your particular purpose. We suggest the following three ways that this book might be read and used:

1. As a regular book

This option is for those of you who read to gather information or to intelligibly enter the conversation with others. If this is you, read straight through the book, skipping the discussion questions and projects.

2. As a spiritual formation workbook

For those who are seeking personal transformation, this option will move you from being passive listeners to active participants. Besides reading through the book, you should engage through the questions and projects.

If you were to wrestle with every question, it would take you hours, even days, to work through a chapter. Instead, read through all the questions and focus on a few that stand out to you. Remember, you aren't being graded on your answers, so don't hold back. The deeper you engage, the greater opportunity you create for transformation.

The same goes for the projects. With between three and five projects per chapter, it would be overwhelming to do all the projects at once. Instead, we encourage you to choose at least one project per chapter. Certain projects will strike a chord more than others, so work on these first; then at a later time, you might be compelled to revisit some of the other projects.

3. As a small group book

We personally think this is the best way to read this book because relationships are integral for both individual and community spiritual growth. This book was created in community, and it speaks about community. By studying this book with others, you will hear other voices, which will aid you in your own journey, and you will aid others in theirs.

For this option, we recommend doing everything from option 2 on your own and then coming together to work through the Small Group Transformation Questions at the end of each chapter. We suggest a ten-session study in which you introduce the book and work through this Introduction in the first session and spend the next nine sessions working through one chapter at a time. If your group is really motivated, you might plan ahead and divide up the questions and projects among the group so you work through the entire book.

BE PART OF THE BIG PICTURE

The truth is there is a big difference between receiving information and being open to God's transformation. Our hope is that this book will become a new medium through which you not only hear the message but embody it together in your everyday lives.

This book contains a lot of conversation-creating information, questions, and projects that will help move your community to experience the content in a way that can't be done by simply reading the words on its pages. *The Samaritan Project* is about action and transformation!

It is time to engage the community in which you live in a new way.

It is time to put all the practices you have been given into the rhythms of daily discipleship.

It is time to move from simply gaining new information to opening ourselves to God's transformation.

The Parable of the Good Samaritan

LUKE 10:25-37

On one occasion an expert in the law stood up to test Jesus. "Teacher," he asked, "what must I do to inherit eternal life?"

"What is written in the Law?" he replied. "How do you read it?"

He answered: "'Love the Lord your God with all your heart and with all your soul and with all your strength and with all your mind'; and, 'Love your neighbor as yourself.'"

"You have answered correctly," Jesus replied. "Do this and you will live."

But he wanted to justify himself, so he asked Jesus, "And who is my neighbor?"

In reply Jesus said: "A man was going down from Jerusalem to Jericho, when he fell into the hands of robbers. They stripped him of his clothes, beat him and went away, leaving him half dead. A priest happened to be going down the same road, and when he saw the man, he passed by on the other side. So too, a Levite, when he came to the place and saw him, passed by on the other side. But a Samaritan, as he traveled, came where the man was; and when he saw him, he took pity on him. He went to him and bandaged his wounds, pouring on oil and wine. Then he put the man on his own donkey, took him to an inn and took care of him. The next day he took out two silver coins and gave them to the innkeeper. 'Look after him,' he said, 'and when I return, I will reimburse you for any extra expense you may have.'

"Which of these three do you think was a neighbor to the man who fell into the hands of robbers?"

The expert in the law replied, "The one who had mercy on him."

Jesus told him, "Go and do likewise."

Chapter One

THE STORY BEGINS

THE IMPORTANCE OF STORY

Most people enjoy a good story. Whether it unfolds on the pages of a dusty classic novel, on a movie screen, or over coffee with a lifelong friend, an engaging narrative has the power to raise us to a better state. Maybe it's because we like losing ourselves, escaping from something or to something. Maybe it's the hope we find in stories; they make us believe that we too might experience a fairytale ending. Or maybe we enjoy stories because they connect us. As we listen to or watch a story unfold, we find parts of ourselves in the narrative—in a character or a setting, in an experience or a pursuit. When we are able to relate to a story, even for a moment, we know we are not alone: we know we are not that different from everyone else after all.

Our lives consist of a compilation of small stories that all contribute to our life story, and our individual life stories combine to tell a larger story of our family, our generation, our nation, and our world. But in a society that has become increasingly disconnected, we don't often think of our lives in this way. Individualism and isolation run rampant in our Western culture. Although we are sophisticated in many areas, when it comes to relationships with our co-workers, our neighbors, perhaps even members of our family, we are lacking. We have exchanged intimacy for popularity and quality for quantity. We are enamored with social networks like Facebook and Twitter, and yet we use them not to connect but rather to stay at arm's length from one another. The way we connect with others and how close we allow them to get to us need to change if we are going to be able to see and experience a grander story.

What would it look like if we embraced a different narrative from the one the world around us offers? What if we could be part of the greatest story ever told? What if we already are part of this story and all we need to do is have our eyes opened to a new reality all around us?

THE GRAND STORY

The Bible is a collection of narratives that all come together to tell a much larger story. We call it the grand story. Like most stories, it has a beginning and an end, characters, a setting, and a plot (crisis) that is moving toward some type of resolution. When we read the individual stories, it is easy to get caught up in the details and miss the point of the grand story as a whole. From these individual narratives, or even from smaller pieces of these narratives, we as the Church have constructed all kinds of rules and doctrines— even heresies. We use some of these constructs to protect us, to isolate us, or to grow our congregations.

Maybe we have missed the point. Maybe we need to take a couple giant steps back and catch the bigger picture—because between Genesis and Revelation lies a story like no other. The *crisis* was introduced very early in the story with the fall of humanity. The *setting* is our world. Look around you. Everything you see is part of the story. God has created it and has given it purpose. In fact, everything and everyone has true purpose only within the story. Our lives don't (and can't) make sense outside of this story because there is actually no reality outside of this grand story. The *resolution* to the story comes in Jesus Christ. He is the crescendo of this story—in his first coming and his coming again.

So the story has not ended, and we're all *characters* in it. From our limited perspectives, we may believe we are the main characters, but the reality is that the story is God's story. Yes, we are included, but only because he includes us.

HIS STORY VERSUS OUR STORY

Most of us spend a great deal of our Christian lives trying to figure out how to fit God's story into our own. We want God in our story, but we are not willing to allow his story to supersede our own, so we compartmentalize our faith in such a way that we allow God to become only a *part* of our lives. But God is so expansive that he quickly tears apart the compartments we have constructed to restrain him.

How can we think that all of who God is, his grand story, can possibly fit inside our story? It would be like trying to wrap the book of my life or your life around an entire thirty-two-volume encyclopedia set. Without a doubt, our binding would be brutally torn to shreds after only a couple volumes. So why do we do it? Maybe it's because we see value in his story but we are afraid of losing ourselves in it. Maybe it's because the world has told us that we are priority one and we believe it.

What if instead of losing ourselves in God's story, we *found* ourselves? This is what happens when we recognize our story as part of his rather than the other way around. And when we begin to view life and Scripture from a grander perspective, the Bible is no longer an old book full of unrelated stories that took place thousands of years ago. Instead, it becomes *our* story. *We* were created by God. *We* are the ones who disobeyed and ate the forbidden fruit, the ones who decided to create our own stories. *We* are the children of Abraham, the covenant people, God's chosen ones. *We* are the ones God delivered from Egypt, from the hands of Pharaoh. *We* are the ones who wandered in the desert for forty years because of our fear, stubbornness, and disobedience. *We* are the ones who entered the Promised Land only to lose it again. *We* are the ones who were exiled and then delivered again. *We* are the ones who God has constantly been seeking, for whom Christ has come, and for whom Christ is coming again.

God's story is our story because he is our God and we are his children. The Bible's individual stories start to make a lot more sense when we recognize our own brokenness in them and our need for a savior. Our own stories also start to make more sense as we recognize that we are not that different from anyone else—that we are all connected through him, whether we know it or accept it. And through it all, God's love and grace and mercy shine through over and over again in the midst of our personal and corporate darkness.

When you were a child, what was your favorite story? To which characters in the story did you most relate? Why?

What is your favorite story from the Scriptures? To which characters and events do you most relate? Why?

Discuss instances when you have tried to fit God's grand story into your individual story instead of the other way around. How did these instances turn out?

Have you ever been afraid that following God might result in you losing yourself? Where do you think that fear comes from?

ENVELOPED IN GOD'S STORY

Write out your story in the form of a time-line. Place important dates and events that you consider to have shaped who you are as a person. You may need to talk to a parent or friend to help you remember some of these things. You can include as much or as little information as you like.

Take your story, fold it up, and place in between the pages of God's story, the Bible. This act places your life, with its joys and pains, in perspective. It is a physical reminder to you that his story has now become your story and your story has become part of God's grand story.

Project

15

THE IMPORTANCE OF COMMUNITY

If everything we have said is true, then embracing God's story means embracing each other's stories as well. In a great quote that is attributed to the Australian Aboriginal Elder Lilla Watson, she says, "If you come here to help me, you're wasting your time. If you come because your liberation is bound up with mine, then let us work together."[1]

In a very real way our stories, and through them our liberation, are "bound up" in each other. We don't mean that we find salvation in or through other people. Salvation comes through an intimate and faithful relationship with God, through Christ, guided by the Spirit, but Scripture makes a very clear connection between our relationship with God and our relationship with each another. Here are just a few examples:

- **Humanity's Creation**: Genesis 1:26-27 tells us that we were created in the *image* and *likeness* of the corporate God (Father, Son and Holy Spirit), and that we were created corporately. Genesis 1:27 reads, "So God created man in his own image, in the image of God he created him; male and female he created them." Genesis 2 tells us that it was "not good for the man to be alone" (v. 18) and that woman was created from man that "they will become one flesh" (v. 24). It seems that from the point of creation, humanity has been innately tied together.

- **Greatest Commandment:** In Matthew 22:37-40 Jesus tells us that the greatest commandment is to love God with all our heart, soul, and mind and to love our neighbors as ourselves. This is an interesting passage since the two commandments are described as one and appear to be inseparable.

- **Love for God = Love for Others:** In 1 John 4:19-20, John writes, "We love because he first loved us. If anyone says, 'I love God,' yet hates his brother, he is a liar. For anyone who does not love his brother, whom he has seen, cannot love God, whom he has not seen." These are some harsh words. And this isn't the only time this idea appears in the Bible. Romans 13:9, Galatians 5:14, and James 2:8 mirror these verses as well.

- **Love for Others = Love for God:** So is the reverse true as well, that loving others is equal to loving God? This appears to be what Jesus alludes to in the Parable of the Sheep and Goats (Matthew 25:31-46). Jesus says that in serving and loving the "least of these" we have served and loved him!

Thus, we see our stories are intertwined and our liberation is brought to fruition in our recognition and service of the other. This is why community is so important. As we said above, our stories are not created in a vacuum. They are united (or at least they should be). This should be truer of the Church than of any other group because our stories are united through God's grand story. In fact, we continue this grand story every time we live out genuine community and every time we extend this story to our neighbors.

But who is our neighbor? Well, this is what this book is all about—discovering ourselves in his story so that we can discover our neighbors and in so doing, be a part of the story.

What do you think God meant when he said that "it is not good for man to be alone?" When have you or do you feel most alone?

In which communities have you felt most at home? Why do you think this was the case?

Why do you think John would say that it is impossible to love God and hate your brother?

Have you ever sensed that in serving someone you were actually serving God? What made you feel that way?

TAKE TIME TO LISTEN

Take some time to listen to another person's story. Ask this person if you can interview him or her to explore the many ways your stories connect. As you listen, pay attention to how this individual's experiences resonate with your own.

Here are a few questions you might ask:

What was the community like where you grew up?

What are your fondest memories of your family while growing up?

What were your dreams when you were a child?

Who are the people who have loved you most in your life?

What do you think is your calling in life?

Project

CONTEXT IS EVERYTHING!

Without context, words and actions have no meaning. In fact, life has no meaning without context. As humans, we tend to forget the importance of context and thus pull things out of it. We take a wild gorilla and put it in a cage in a zoo in the middle of a city and wonder why it seems unhappy or becomes aggressive. We take a phrase uttered by a politician and use it against him or her even though the phrase had a completely different meaning when it was spoken. We take passages of scripture and use them to justify our actions even though in their contexts they have nothing to do with how we are using them. For this reason, it is important to understand the context of our story as a whole.

As the Scriptures demonstrate, stories are often layered and complex. For instance, the Parable of the Good Samaritan is a story in and of itself and yet it is only one part of a larger story—the story of Jesus and the inquisitive expert in the law. This story is part of an even larger story of Jesus' ministry as presented in the Gospel according to Luke. And Luke's story is only one viewpoint of the Jesus story, which in and of itself is part of the grand story of God, his people and his redemptive plan for us. We could even add that Scripture is only a piece of the grandest story, a story that no book or volume of books could contain nor human words describe.

To better understand the importance of context, let's consider Luke 9:51 through 10:42 (it wouldn't hurt to re-read this section). A lot is going on beyond what is presented to us. First, at the time of this passage, a major shift has taken place in Jesus' story. Jesus has recognized that the time for his earthly ministry to end is drawing near; therefore, he sets out for Jerusalem to face his impending death. Thus, the story has begun to climax and no doubt tensions are high for Jesus and his disciples (see Luke 9:54-56, for example). Second, this shift has launched a focused teaching on discipleship. Jesus knows he will be leaving soon, and he wants to make sure his followers know exactly what it means to be a disciple after he is gone. For this reason, in this passage Luke seems to stress examples of what to do and what not to do. The lawyer represents the negative example and the Samaritan the positive example. In the same way, Martha represents the negative example and Mary the positive one (10:38-42).

These very simple and brief contextual clues help us read our story with more accuracy and therefore help us better understand what Jesus was trying to teach his disciples, the lawyer, Martha, and us. In Luke's story of Mary and Martha, Martha is so concerned about pleasing Jesus and providing for him that she doesn't even take the time to just *be* with him. Mary, on the other hand, recognizes this once-in-a-lifetime opportunity to sit in the presence of the Savior and listen. Jesus' response to Martha's frustration speaks volumes into our story.

The lawyer in our story, like Martha, is caught up in *doing* rather than in *being*. This is part of the reason he needs to justify himself by asking the question about who qualifies as his neighbor. At worst, he is attempting to control the conversation: at best, he is trying to figure out what he has to *do* in order to inherit eternal life. Either way, he misses the point! The Samaritan, like Mary, isn't concerned about his own safety or his own salvation. He isn't even concerned about *doing* the right thing (even though he does). The Samaritan acts out of who he is and what he knows. He is *being* a neighbor and in so doing, he is living out love for God and love for his neighbor at the same time.

By considering context, we see that these two very different episodes are linked together, and we see the heart of our parable is not about commandments or earning eternal life. It is not about what we must do or not do. It is about sitting in God's presence and listening to his Spirit speak to us in order that we might be the kind of people who do good and right things simply out of *being* who we are in Christ.

React to this thought: "Without context, words and actions have no meaning. In fact, life has no meaning without context." What does this statement mean to you? Do you agree or disagree? Why?

Think of a time when someone took something you said out of context. How did it make you feel? How was the situation resolved?

Have you ever overreacted in a situation because you were unaware of the bigger picture? Discuss your experience.

How does the context of this parable help shape your understanding?

What is your current context (your social and cultural setting; the places, things, and people that influence you; your belief system)? How does your context shape you?

Questions

MISQUOTED

Take an opportunity to read a news article or watch a TV news report in which someone says he or she was misquoted. You can simply Google "misquoted" to find an example. You may also use a passage of Scripture or a sermon. Your example could be about politics, sports, religion, or entertainment. Look at the comments that the speaker was credited with making, and then look to find the larger context of what he or she was saying. Now that you have a broader perspective, do you agree that the individual's comments were taken out of context? How important is it to know the context before you pass judgment on someone?

CONCLUSION

We live in a world that judges people's value based on what they do or what they add to the household, the business, or our world as a whole. For this reason, we spend much of our time trying to write our own stories. If we can just make a mark for ourselves, leave a legacy, then others will respect and remember us. Then we will be worth something. Then we will be happy or fulfilled.

But Christ, and Scripture as a whole, paints a different picture of success. Success lies in finding ourselves in his story. Success is learning to be his. It is about learning to belong to a community that is being transformed into Christ's image. No story we create for ourselves will ever be as great as the one to which he has invited us to be a part. We only have to join the story.

BENEDICTION

Now, may the God who spoke the story into existence be allowed to permeate your story with his. May you learn what it means to be his and to operate out of this being. May you find yourself in a community in which you learn to let go of your tendency to isolate yourself and embrace the world around you as part of his body.

What is the first story you remember hearing? Or, what is your earliest memory? Why did either of these stay with you?

Why do you think stories have such a powerful impact?

Outside of the Christian grand narrative, what other grand stories shape the way people live?

Think about the passages that were mentioned regarding the connection between loving God and loving his creation. When did you first recognize this important relationship? How does this realization shape the way you live?

If you chose the project "Take Time to Listen," take a few moments to share your experience. Why did you choose the person you interviewed? Which of their answers resonated with you? Which of their answers surprised you?

Think about the importance of context. Have your words ever been taken out of context? Did this situation affect any of your relationships? How was the situation resolved?

Read Luke 10:25-42. What role do you think this story plays in the larger narrative of Luke's Gospel?

Discuss some of the projects you worked on in this chapter. How did God transform you through them? How did they help you better understand the story, yourself, others, and the world around you?

Small Group

TRANSFORMATION QUESTIONS

Chapter Two

WHY ASK WHY?

"MIRROR, MIRROR ON THE WALL"

Mirrors have been around for thousands of years. Even before people began to shape materials into reflective tools, it is believed that our ancient ancestors stared into quiet pools or tubs of still water in order to see themselves. The oldest known mirrors were created around 6000 BC in what is now Turkey and were made of volcanic glass. In ancient Egypt, it is believed that these reflective devices were used in religious rituals as symbols representing the sun and the moon.[1]

While mirrors are now used in cameras, telescopes, and lasers, their primary use through the centuries has been to show us our reflections. In fact, there is a lot of superstition about the images we find in mirrors. Some have said that mirrors not only reflect one's image, but they have the power to reflect one's soul or transport one to another world. This superstition has been the subject of films and stories like *Alice in Wonderland* and *Snow White*.

While most of us do not believe in these superstitions, we do trust mirrors on a daily basis to give us the best representation of how we look before we head out into the world. The reflective power of a mirror can be a potent apparatus for helping form not only our personal appearance but the appearance of our surroundings. For instance, mirrors are valuable tools in interior decorating: the simplest solution to make a room seem larger is to add a mirror. In this way, mirrors are like questions. Just as a mirror creates space when hung on a blank wall, a properly positioned question can create opportunity for a world of possibility, taking all the tension and tightness out of an enclosed space.

As we will see, some of the most potent texts in Scripture are those in which the authors insert a question like a mirror on a blank wall. As we think about our passage, let's use the reflective power of the mirror as an illustration of the reflective power of the questions we encounter in Scripture—particularly in the story of the Good Samaritan.

"WHERE ARE YOU?"

In Genesis 3, Adam and Eve waste no time eating from the one tree in all of creation that God had commanded them was off limits. Even though they have disobeyed God, they know they will have to engage him when he meets them for their daily walk. So, they hide:

> Then the man and his wife heard the sound of the LORD God as he was walking in the garden in the cool of the day, and they hid from the LORD God among the trees of the garden. But the LORD God called to the man, "Where are you?" (Genesis 3:8-9)

Of course, God is aware of both their location and their act of disobedience, but rather than arriving on the scene in a rage because they have not obeyed, he walks in patiently. He doesn't start with accusations; instead, God offers up a question—"Where are you?" It is a moment of pause. A moment for the guilty party to respond. A moment to engage before the inevitable defensiveness sets in. It is a moment to take account of oneself before the guilty party tucks tail and retreats as quickly as possible. It is here in this question that we see the posture of our merciful God on display for the first time. In the midst of humanity's utter and tragic failure, God wants us to know that his first move is not condemnation but conversation.

* * *

Throughout the Scriptures there are numerous texts in which God's questions express his patience with us. How about Job when he has finally experienced more tragedy than his soul can bear? Job's frustration reminds us of those times when we begin to think that the tragic circumstances of our lives are the proof that this all-powerful God really has no idea what he is doing "up there." It is then that God questions Job, asking, "'Where were you when I laid the earth's foundation'" (Job 38:4)?

In Genesis 4, Cain and his brother go out to the field, but only one of them comes back. God, fully aware that Cain has planted his brother six feet deep, enters the situation by asking him, "'Where is your brother Abel'" (v. 9)? In Genesis 32, Jacob, the liar and thief, is found wrestling with God. Before the match ends in a draw, Jacob requests that God bless him. God responds, asking Jacob, "'What is your name'" (v. 27)? For most of us this is a simple request. But for a man named "deceiver," who has lived his whole life embodying this name, answering God's question requires a bit more honesty than even we might want to admit.

Later in the Bible, we encounter Isaiah, standing in awe, being confronted with the question, "'Whom shall I send? And who will go for us?'" (Isaiah 6:8). And in 1 Kings 19, after Elijah has just defeated the priests of Baal and incurred the wrath of the queen, we find him hiding out in a cave. It is at this low point that God enters with water, food, and a question: "'What are you doing here, Elijah?'" (1 Kings 19:9, 13).

Throughout the Bible we see the power of questions to offer us a means to see our own reflection. In the midst of these stories of human folly and frailty, God enters in and tries to approach us in a way that opens dialogue. From Adam hiding in shame to Elijah running in fear, we see the image of a God who hopes that the opening of a conversation might possibly bring healing and restore courage in a way that a word of rebuke or rejection never could. God understands that in these situations a question can create more awareness than any "statement" would ever be able to achieve.

Do you think questions are helpful? When was the last time someone asked you a helpful question?

What is the purpose of questions in Scripture? What do they accomplish?

React to this line: "In the midst of humanity's utter and tragic failure, God wants us to know that his first move is not condemnation but conversation."

Who asks you tough questions that make you reflect? Of whom do you ask tough questions?

Questions

GETTING BEHIND THE QUESTIONS

Think of the last few days. What questions have you asked? List some of them and reflect on why you asked them. Were they meant to help you gain information, or possibly to get a material item? Did you ask any questions as a means of slowing down a situation or to encourage someone to reflect for a moment?

Project

A QUESTION IS WORTH A THOUSAND WORDS

A tourist walks into an art gallery while on vacation. The woman, after taking time to peruse the artwork, turns to the shop owner, who is also the artist, and asks, "Which one is your favorite?" The painter pauses for a moment, takes a look around his shop, and responds with a question of his own: "Do you have children?" At first the woman is confused by such a strange response but engages the painter, replying, "Yes, I have a son and two daughters." The painter then asks her, "Which one is your favorite?"

This illustration reminds us that sometimes questions can be more telling than answers. In Scripture, this is often the case. In fact, the Parable of the Good Samaritan actually begins with a question, when Jesus is engaged by an expert in the law who is trying to get to the bottom of who he really is. In order to do this, the expert asks a particularly telling question, one that will expose the stance of any teacher of the Hebrew faith: "'Teacher,' he ask[s], 'what must I do to inherit eternal life'" (Luke 10:25)?

When we look at this passage, it's important for us to understand a bit about this particular question. The expert in the law is a Jewish authority, a person with (as the word "expert" suggests), a deep knowledge of the law. When he asks about "eternal life," he probably does not have in mind many of the images that enter ours. He is not thinking about some sort of escape from the earth to a far off distant heaven after he dies. More likely he is thinking like a typical first-century Jew.

In his cultural context, the term "eternal life" was used to separate the idea that there was a present age but also an age to come in which God would reveal his kingdom of peace and justice to the world (take a look at Isaiah 2:1-4). So, the expert is asking, "How do I make sure that when God's reign begins, I will not miss out on being a part of it?" Similar to our world today, there were many perspectives on what was required to inherit eternal life.

Confronted with this question, Jesus can respond in a number of different ways. He can give the expert a list of answers about how to prepare, he can run and hide recognizing this as a trap, or he can do what he actually does—offer a question, a mirror: "'What is written in the Law?' he [replies]. 'How do you read it'" (Luke 10:26)? The expert in the law responds with,

> "'Love the Lord your God with all your heart and with all your soul and with all your strength and with all your mind'; and, 'Love your neighbor as yourself.'" "You have answered correctly," Jesus [replies]. "Do this and you will live." But he want[s] to justify himself, so he ask[s] Jesus, "And who is my neighbor?" (Luke 10:27-29)

The expert's unhealthy confidence and contentment in his own perspective prevent him from grasping what Jesus is trying to tell him. In his rebuttal question for Jesus, he reveals that he seeks not to understand but rather to "justify himself." Like the expert, we are often content with the reflection we already have of ourselves. When this perspective is challenged, we become defensive and lash out with our own questions, but our questions do not offer the opportunity for insight or growth. They do not allow us to move outside of ourselves.

What is the best question you have ever been asked? Why?

Do you think questions can be as formative as answers?

Have you ever felt "trapped" in a conversation? How did you respond?

FEARFULLY AND WONDERFULLY MADE

Stand in front of a mirror and read Psalm 139 as a prayer. What lines stand out to you as you read the text while viewing your own reflection? What do you think it means to be "fearfully and wonderfully made?" How do you feel when you look in a mirror? Why do you think you feel that way? What questions do you hear God asking you as you look in the mirror?

PSALM 139

O LORD, you have searched me
and you know me.
You know when I sit and when I rise;
you perceive my thoughts from afar.
You discern my going out and my lying down;
you are familiar with all my ways.
Before a word is on my tongue
you know it completely, O LORD.

You hem me in—behind and before;
you have laid your hand upon me.
Such knowledge is too wonderful for me,
too lofty for me to attain.

Where can I go from your Spirit?
Where can I flee from your presence?
If I go up to the heavens, you are there;
if I make my bed in the depths, you are there.
If I rise on the wings of the dawn,
if I settle on the far side of the sea,
even there your hand will guide me,
your right hand will hold me fast.

If I say, "Surely the darkness will hide me
and the light become night around me,"
even the darkness will not be dark to you;
the night will shine like the day,
for darkness is as light to you.

For you created my inmost being;
    you knit me together in my mother's
        womb.
I praise you because I am fearfully and
        wonderfully made;
    your works are wonderful,
    I know that full well.
My frame was not hidden from you
    when I was made in the secret place.
When I was woven together in the depths
        of the earth,
    your eyes saw my unformed body.
All the days ordained for me
    were written in your book
    before one of them came to be.

How precious to me are your thoughts, O
        God!
    How vast is the sum of them!
Were I to count them,
    they would outnumber the grains of
        sand.
When I awake,
    I am still with you.

If only you would slay the wicked, O God!
    Away from me, you bloodthirsty men!
They speak of you with evil intent;
    your adversaries misuse your name.
Do I not hate those who hate you, O LORD,
    and abhor those who rise up against you?
I have nothing but hatred for them;
    I count them my enemies.

Search me, O God, and know my heart;
    test me and know my anxious thoughts.
See if there is any offensive way in me,
    and lead me in the way everlasting.

QUESTIONS AS WINDOWS

For a moment let's go back to our interior decorating illustration. The much more expensive, but also much more expansive, way to create space in a room is to add a window. Cutting a window into an empty wall opens up the opportunity not for self-reflecting but for re-envisioning. Seeing through a new window can open us up to a world we could not have seen or imagined before. In the case of the encounter between the expert and Jesus, the final question Jesus asks serves as a window that challenges the expert to view a new world altogether.

> "'Which of these three do you think was a neighbor to the man who fell into the hands of robbers'" (Luke 10:36)?

Jesus reshapes a question that was originally meant to *justify* its asker into a question that has the purpose and possibility to *transform* the asker. Jesus recognizes the intention of the expert's question, but he does not respond in defensiveness or destruction or simply end the conversation. Instead, Jesus returns the question in a deeper form than the asker had ever expected, transforming the idea of "neighbor" from a noun to a verb. Through this interaction the expert is given the opportunity to re-envision his idea of love and neighbor.

On April 3, 1968, Dr. Martin Luther King, Jr. delivered his famous "I've Been to the Mountaintop" speech at Bishop Charles Mason Temple in Memphis, Tennessee. In what would be his final address, he used the parable of the Good Samaritan as his text. Dr. King described his firsthand experience of driving down from Jerusalem to Jericho and his witness to how dangerous this road really was. It would have been a perfect setting to ambush pedestrian travelers. King then went on to describe motivations of the priests in our story. He agreed that there was no certainty as to why the religious leaders did not stop to help the man. He did believe though, there was at least an insight into how they dealt with the dilemma. King stated, "The first question that the priest asked, the first question that the Levite asked was, 'If I stop to help this man, what will happen to me?'"[2] King recognized that the action of distancing themselves from the beaten man at the side of the road expressed their concern for self-preservation, despite whether their motivation was based on purity or safety. But then Dr. King suggested that the question on the heart and mind of the Good Samaritan completely reversed that of the religious leaders'. For the Samaritan the question was, "'If I do not stop to help this man, what will happen to *him*?'"[3]

Dr. King recognized that the question the Levite and the priest asked themselves never moved them beyond concerns of self-preservation. The question the Samaritan asked himself, though, forced him to move outside of himself to the place where he could see himself and the world from a different perspective.

· · ·

In the film *Hotel Rwanda* there is an exchange between Paul Rusesabagina (Don Cheadle) and a videographer, Jack Daglish (Joaquin Phoenix). While Jack is editing footage of the atrocities of the genocides in Rwanda, which he is preparing to send out for broadcast, Paul accidently walks in on him. The following conversation takes place later when Paul encounters Jack in the hotel restaurant.

> **Jack Daglish**: Listen. Sorry about earlier. If I had known that you were in there, I wouldn't have . . .
>
> **Paul Rusesabagina**: I am glad that you have shot this footage and that the world will see it. It is the only way we have a chance that people might intervene.
>
> **Jack Daglish**: Yeah, and if no one intervenes, is it still a good thing to show?
>
> **Paul Rusesabagina**: How can they not intervene when they witness such atrocities?
>
> **Jack Daglish**: I think if people see this footage they'll say, "Oh, my God, that's horrible," and then go on eating their dinners.[4]

This scene from the film is a great example of the insulation we put up around ourselves. Jack suggests that most of the world, even when confronted with the violent and horrific images of genocide, will not be moved to any sense of real action. Like the Levite and the priest, we are able to look at those in desperate situations while still keeping our distance. We tend to ask the self-portrait question, never looking at ourselves as we really are, never being able to see the world outside our room. Never realizing that we aren't the main characters in God's story.

In the film, Paul Rusesabagina is made out to be a man from the right tribe, a man with the connections and means, a man who, if he had just settled on self-preservation, could have gotten out of the difficulties of the tragedy. But instead, he continues to follow the example of the Samaritan, asking, "If I leave, what will happen to my family, my neighbors, those in need?"

What do you think is the difference between the question the expert in the law asks and the one Jesus asks after the story of the Good Samaritan?

What do you think is the difference between the two questions that Dr. King suggests the characters ask in the story of the Good Samaritan?

Think of the last time you were faced with a situation that required you to choose between self-preservation and self-sacrifice. How was the situation resolved?

When we do not help someone in trouble, are we adding to the problem? Are we becoming part of the cause of the trouble? Why or why not?

Questions

CHARACTER EVALUATION

Watch the film *Hotel Rwanda* (or a similar film regarding a major conflict, such as *The Killing Fields*, *Swing Kids*, *Schindler's List*, or *Blood Diamond*). What is the tragedy or crisis around which the film revolves? Which characters benefit the most from the conflict? Which characters suffer the most from the conflict? Which characters act the most in regards to self-preservation? Which characters make the most sacrifices in order to preserve others?

CONCLUSION

As we've discussed throughout this chapter, just as we utilize mirrors as a means to see ourselves and use windows as a means to see the world around us, a well-placed question can enable us to reflect on our actions and intentions. Asking good questions can also open up a window into the world that lies outside of us—offering a view that we were unable to see before. In our next chapter we will begin to look into the lives of each of the characters in Jesus' story. As we do, remember the power of questioning where you see yourself in our story.

In the end, following in the way of Jesus requires us to re-imagine how we have conversations. When we follow Jesus, we re-envision the power of conversation to not only be a means of giving and receiving information, but a means to transform relationships. So is it possible that the next time we pose the question, "How are you?" we might actually pause long enough to hear the answer? Is it possible that the next time someone does not meet our expectations, our first response might not be a word of anger or judgment but a question of patience and possibility?

Maybe in asking good questions today, we will be able to offer others the grace of a mirror or a window to expand their view of themselves or the world outside.

BENEDICTION

Now, may God teach us to be a people of honesty and openness. May we be honest about the questions that both challenge and transform us. May we be open to the power of the Spirit's questioning and leading. May we be people today who have the courage to ask and receive good questions. Amen.

How much time do you spend in front of a mirror each day? Do you think it is possible to spend too much time in front of the mirror?

Who are the people who ask you questions that cause you to reflect?

What is one of your favorite questions that God asks in the Scriptures? Why?

What do you think the expert meant by his question, "Who is my neighbor?" What do you think it means to justify oneself?

Can you remember a time when you asked a question as a means of justifying yourself?

Think back to the questions you have asked in the past twenty-four hours. Were any of your questions asked as a means of providing a mirror or a window to a situation? If not, look back and reflect on whether any of those situations could have been.

Discuss some of the projects you worked on in this chapter. How did God transform you through them? How did they help you better understand the story, yourself, others, and the world around you?

Small Group

TRANSFORMATION QUESTIONS

Chapter Three

UNDERSTANDING OURSELVES IN THE STORY

THE HERO

Children are much better at embracing story than we adults are. In fact, they live in a world of stories, a world in which each new day brings new adventures. Theirs is a blending of reality and make-believe. After all, there are endless possibilities when a blanket is a cape, a stuffed animal is a fellow adventurer, and each room is a cave, a forest, or a mountaintop. Children may not fully understand right from wrong or good from bad and yet they do know they want to be the victorious hero in each and every game they play. Why is this? And do we ever outgrow this tendency?

Maybe the problem we face as adults is that even as life becomes increasingly more complex, we continue to hold on to simple constructs that no longer prove possible or helpful. For instance, we read the parable of the Good Samaritan and automatically try to transport ourselves into the place of the Samaritan. He is the hero after all, right? But what happens when our own lives look more like the priest or the Levite—when we feel we are anything but the hero? The natural reaction in this case is for us to distance ourselves from the story altogether. We turn the parable into prose and pull out whatever practical instruction we can glean after discarding the "fluff." But by reading this story and the rest of the Bible as stand-alone passages from which we can pull out what we like and reject what makes us uncomfortable, we risk not fully understanding what it means to be part of God's story.

What if it is just as important to understand how we are the villain, the victim, or the viewer in the Samaritan story? What if we can move past the labels and embrace the good, the bad, and the ugly of who we are? What if we can learn to accept the possibilities and the hope and the grace of God as we find ourselves more and more in God's story?

With roughly 6.9 billion people in the world, it probably won't take us long to realize we can't all be the hero in every situation. Of course, we can try to define hero in ways that make us feel better about who we are and what we do, but doing so won't really change anything—and won't change us. Only when we stop believing we are always the hero and begin to realize that Christ is the only true hero and one of the main characters in God's story can we be transformed into his image.

LIVING IN THE PRESENT

In a great quote by German theologian Jürgen Moltmann, he writes:

> Memory binds him [humanity] to the past that no longer is. Hope casts him upon the future that is not yet. . . . He hopes to live, but he does not live. He expects to be happy one day, and this expectation causes him to pass over the happiness of the present. He is never, in memory and hope, wholly himself and wholly in his present.[1]

How true is this? We spend most of our time living in the past or chasing the future and because of this, we miss the present. We miss all that God is doing in and through us right here and right now.

Hope is a great thing. In fact, it is one of the greatest gifts God has given us. But when our hope is not grounded in the present, we end up chasing empty dreams or unrealistic expectations. How might we learn from the past while still living in the present and at the same time keeping our focus on the future reality toward which God is moving us? And how does all this relate to our story?

It's simple. Most of us read this parable and either try to run from the reality that we have often been the priest or the Levite or try to picture a way we might become the Good Samaritan. All the while, God wants to use our present circumstances to transform us. God is most concerned about our present—not about what we *have* done or *have* been nor about what we *will* be or *will* do. Why is this? Because relationships are lived out in the present! Therefore, we must embrace the present opportunities to live out this relationship with Christ in the midst of his story. In the present, we must try to discover who we are, how we got there, and how God is trying to move and shape us. The Parable of the Good Samaritan is one of many biblical stories that can help us do just that. Yet, we must remember that life is more complex and multi-dimensional than how we normally read this story. Therefore, if we hope to be transformed, we will need to delve a little deeper.

In the pages that follow, we have evaluated the individual characters in the parable. But please don't get caught up in the titles and miss the point. Our hope is that in creating these categories, we will be able to target a particular learned action (or reaction) and what's behind this action (or reaction). Once we discover and claim present realities of who we are and how we act in a particular situation, we can begin to ask ourselves the difficult questions that will ultimately move us toward transformation and growth in our relationship with Christ.

THE AVOIDER

The priest and the Levite both represent the avoider. These two religious leaders come across a badly beaten man and do nothing to help him. Instead, they move to the other side of the road and continue on their way. When we first hear this part of the story, we are outraged. "How could they do this?" "Didn't they have any compassion?" "Hypocrites!" We quickly pass judgment on these heartless, religious elitists—as they have often been branded. But is our judgment warranted? Maybe, instead, we should be trying to discover the motivation behind their avoidance or the worldview that gave way to this motivation.

It has been widely assumed that these religious leaders avoided the beaten man because they feared he was dead. If this were the case, then coming in contact with him would have meant their instant impurity (see Leviticus 21:1-3). If they became unclean, they would be unable to carry out their religious duties. Maybe, then, they thought that they would be able to help more people if they remained clean. After all, this was the task to which God had called them in the first place.

We'll never know for sure why the priest passed by the beaten man: in trying to uncover and infer his motive, we risk missing an important opportunity to find ourselves at this place in the story. Consider the times we have avoided the homeless man holding a cardboard sign or the times we have seen friends in need and done nothing. Or what about the times when our motives were pure but we still missed the point? How many times have we put work before friends and family because we thought we were doing more good by getting ourselves into an improved financial state where we might better provide for these people? How many times have we made what we thought was the right decision, only to find out it caused more harm than good? Only when we honestly consider these instances in our own lives can we begin to understand that this type of motivation may have been at the root of the priest's and the Levite's avoidance.

Of course, it's possible that the priest's and the Levite's motives were entirely selfish. Maybe one of them got woozy at the sight of blood. Maybe one of them was afraid that the same people who beat this man were still lurking in the shadows waiting for their next victim. Maybe one of them was late for an appointment. Just maybe, they were completely indifferent to the needs of anyone but themselves. We don't know their story. But we do know ours!

Depending on how we respond to them, moments like these can either be transformative or totally uneventful. When we learn to recognize the attitudes, actions, and reactions that cause us to avoid situations that make us uncomfortable, we stop avoiding these particular situations and embrace them as opportunities to grow and, more importantly, to be Christ to those around us. We may find a justifiable reason for our avoidance (we discuss this issue in Chapter 5), or we may find a history of learned reactions that we need to address. Either way, we will have taken steps toward transformation—which is never a bad thing.

Do people generally think of you as a compassionate person? Why or why not?

What people or places do those in your community commonly avoid because they are afraid? What places or peoples do you avoid on a daily basis?

Questions

When you pass by someone who is stranded on a main road or highway, what do you say to yourself to justify passing by?

Project

TAKE FIFTEEN

Think about someone you avoid on a regular basis: it may be a coworker, a fellow student or a homeless person in your community. Take fifteen minutes this week to engage this individual or group of people, in conversation. If it is a coworker, invite him or her for a cup of coffee. If it is a fellow student, share a meal together. If it is a homeless person, offer to buy him or her a meal. The key is to engage someone you would ordinarily choose to avoid. Then, journal about your experience. Why do you ordinarily avoid this person? Has engaging him or her changed your opinion—either of yourself or this person?

THE WOUNDED

The wounded man plays a passive yet pivotal role in our story. Indeed, we would not have a story or a "hero" if it weren't for this man. The wounded man reminds us of our own brokenness. He reminds us that pain and suffering are natural parts of the human plight. In a very real way, this plight is part of what connects us to each other. But we need to remember that God did not create us for suffering. He created us for relationship and gave us free will. It was this very gift and our own selfishness that resulted in sin. Now the effects of sin are all around us, and we find ourselves living in a world filled with injustice, where money, power, and war appear to be our gods.

The inevitable result of this devaluing of life is wounded people. Thankfully, though, this isn't the full story. The plot has twisted and the end of the story is already shaping out to be very different from the reality with which we are currently faced. What is even more exciting is that the present can also look very different since God's kingdom has broken into this world and is already transforming it. As odd as it may sound, those who are wounded (or have been wounded) have some of the greatest opportunities to see this new kingdom. As the apostle Paul reminded us, Christ's power is made perfect in our weakness (see 2 Corinthians 12:9).

Each of us has been the wounded one before. For some, this is a chronic condition. While we don't know much about the wounded man in our story, we all know plenty about being wounded. We know that we often cause our own wounds through what we do or don't do or through the situations in which we place ourselves. We know that sometimes others cause our wounds and that some of the deepest wounds come from those closest to us. Finally, we know that some wounds appear to have no explanation apart from our being part of a wounded creation.

When we come face to face with pain and brokenness in our own lives, we have several possibilities. We can run. We can give up. We can pretend it doesn't exist. Or we can embrace it. We know what you're thinking: *Who wants to embrace their wounds?* Of course, none of us does. But maybe this is a result of the fall. Maybe we won't be able to truly move past these wounds until we have embraced them and learned from them. Some people say history repeats itself. This is true for all of us to some degree: when we don't learn from our past mistakes, we keep reliving them over and over.

God taught his people this lesson when they were exiled in Babylon because of their depravity and unrepentant hearts. Through the prophet Jeremiah, God gave the exiles a very shocking message. The heart of this message was *remain*. As you can imagine, staying put was the last thing these people wanted to do. God had promised them a land flowing with milk and honey: after tasting the fruits of this land, they now found themselves far away in a land that was not their own—as slaves to a foreign king. They found themselves in the midst of their own self-inflicted woundedness.

And God's message to them was *remain*. In fact, he actually told them to get comfortable and to seek the welfare of their enemies. He told them that their healing and happiness, their own welfare and freedom, would actually come in the very place of their woundedness. They wanted to run from their wounds. They wanted to give up. They wanted to pretend that God would rescue them even though they hadn't done anything to change. But God knew they must work through their woundedness in order to break free from the cycle. He knows this is true for us as well.

Our greatest comfort in all this is that we don't have to remain in our brokenness alone. God has given us a spirit that cries out *for* us and a body—the Church—that cries out *with* us. So take a hand and hold on. Embrace your woundedness and learn and grow and be transformed.

What do you think about the saying that "it is better to give than to receive?" And which is more difficult for you? Why?

What do you think is the greatest wound you have ever embraced in your life?

Do you ever find it hard to share your needs with others? With whom are you able to share your wounds?

How have you learned from your wounds in the past? How can this help you in your present woundedness?

Questions

COMING TO GRIPS

Do you love Christmas movies? Many of the great Christmas films center around the willingness of the protagonists to come to grips with their own woundedness.

For example: In the film *The Family Man*, Nicolas Cage plays Jack Campbell, a corporate lawyer who cares only about cashing in on the next deal. During the movie we learn that Jack has given up Kate, his college sweetheart, in order to pursue money, power, and the lifestyle they can afford him. Around Christmas, Jack is given a magical glimpse into how his life would be different if he had married Kate and they had raised a family together. At first, he resents the simple life and the burdens of parenting and marriage, but throughout the course of the film, he begins to sense that something is missing from his rich bachelor existence.

Watch one of the following Christmas films and look for the characters who discover their own woundedness throughout the course of the film.

- *The Family Man*
- *Elf*
- *Home Alone*
- *Miracle on 34th Street*
- *It's a Wonderful Life*

THE HELPER

The Samaritan is our "helper;" thus, his actions and motives are the ones we are called to emulate. Unlike the other three characters in our story, the Samaritan plays an active role. This is important because we learn right from the start that if we are going to *be* a "neighbor," we will have to *do* something. But before the *doing* comes the *being*.

Our text tells us the Samaritan "took pity on" or "felt compassion for" the beaten man. Neither of these translations gets to the heart of the matter. The Greek word can more literally be translated as "his bowels were moved" (however, this might be a good argument against using an overly literal translation). At the time this passage was written, the bowels were thought to be the place from whence love and pity originated. Though this understanding is obsolete, the imagery is still valid. Haven't you ever seen or heard something so heart-wrenching or disturbing that you felt your stomach tighten up? What's even more fascinating is that this Greek word is a passive verb. What does that mean for us? It means that compassion is an action (verb) that is brought about by an outside agent (passive). The Samaritan's compassion was an extension of who he was inside, his very being. In the same way, before we can truly act out of God's love, we must be open to this transforming love in our own lives.

Motivation is huge! And our motivations are not always as wholesome as the Samaritan's. We *do* "good" things for all sorts of reasons. Because we feel obligated. Because we want to be accepted. Because we enjoy the way doing good things makes us feel. The world definitely needs *doers*, but it needs *be-ers* more—people who have been radically transformed from the inside and who, therefore, seek to radically transform the world outside. This kind of *doing* will change us—and the world.

The Samaritan doesn't represent a single individual but rather the whole Church. As individuals, we often fall prey to the egocentric motivations mentioned above, but the community of believers is called to be our collective conscience; it safeguards us from ourselves. The Church has not always been the best at this, but that's because the Church has often gotten caught up in *doing* rather than *being*. But we must never give up on the Church, which is a collection of individuals: as Christ transforms individuals, the body will also begin to look and act very differently.

These words by Stanley Hauerwas and William Willimon speak volumes to the *doer* in each of us: The "church knows that its most credible form of witness (and the most 'effective' thing it can do for the world) is the actual creation of a living, breathing, visible community of faith."[2] Yes, we all want to be the "helper," but we can most help ourselves, the body, and the world when we are moved by the Spirit of God. When we learn to belong to Christ and to each other, we will be able to practice relationship in tangible ways that resemble the actions of the Good Samaritan.

When was the last time you sensed
compassion in your heart? What did you
do about it?

Who is the most generous person you
know? Why makes this person generous?
Where does this generosity come from?

Who was the last person you helped? What
did you do? How did it feel?

When was the last time you gave
something anonymously? What did you
give? Why did you give it without mention?
(This question might be a good one to
consider internally or journal about rather
than sharing with a group.)

Project

PRAYER OF COMPASSION

Think about the world in which you live. What social concern moves you to compassion? Your project is to take the next week and offer this prayer to God three times a day—once in the morning, once in the afternoon, and once at night:

> God, I thank you for moving me to compassion about _____.
> I trust that you not only recognize this need in the world but that you are concerned even more than I am. I ask that you would show me ways I will need to change in order to bring about your dream for the world in this area of concern. Amen.

THE OBSERVER

Though the innkeeper plays a relatively small part in the Good Samaritan parable, he represents many of us. In a world obsessed with being entertained, it is not surprising that most of us are perfectly content with being the observer. We live vicariously through the many fictional and non-fictional characters we watch on television and read about in books. We live through the experiences of our friends, our children or other family members, and our co-workers. As a result, we fail to become active participants in our own lives and the lives of those around us.

There are several reasons we fail to act. Many of us are scared. We fear being hurt, being changed, being rejected. We think that if we live life at a distance, we can escape its difficulties. Some of us are simply unmotivated (read: lazy). In short, we have become comfortable with the status quo and unwilling to exert the energy needed to be more than we currently are. Some of us are simply unaware of how much God wants to do in and through us.

We must observe the Samaritans around us before we can catch a vision for something beyond us. Once again, this is not about pointing out our failures but rather about recognizing when and where in our lives we are prone to settle for being the observer. It is only after we claim present realities that we can move past them. Most of us *observe* before we *do*; what is most important is what we do with what we observe. This is why we are so intrigued by the innkeeper in the story. We have so many questions for him:

> *What were you thinking when you saw the Samaritan coming in with the wounded man?*
>
> *When you found out he didn't know this man, did you ask him why he was helping him? How did he respond?*
>
> *Did you charge the Samaritan more money when he came back through to check on the wounded man, or did you cover the cost?*
>
> *How did this event change you? Did the Samaritan's actions influence you to do the same for someone else?*

God allows us to observe amazing events and people all the time. They are not the things or people we read about on news sites or hear about on TV. Rather, they are the things that our world sees as ordinary or average. It is the woman who spends her time helping her elderly neighbor around the house. It is the man who sets time aside each week to mentor the teenage boy who doesn't have a dad. It is that same teenager who volunteers his own time to play basketball with the elementary kids after school. It is the child who spends her allowance on school supplies and toys for a shoebox that will be sent to a child who has nothing. Do we see these people? Do we recognize God working in and through them? Do we understand how their simple acts of love and sacrifice can shape our actions as well?

In a very real way, we are all observers of this story. Like the innkeeper, we have had this story unfold right in front of us; now we are challenged to do something with what we have seen. What will be our next step? Will we walk away unchanged, or will we look inward and move outward?

Who are the models of compassion you have seen in your life?

Who are the people who have involved you in their projects of mercy?

If you could join any social movement in the world, which one would it be? Why?

Questions

LEARNING YOUR CITY

List five great service organizations in your city. If you don't know five, go to your city's website and look up the local non-profits in your community. Take your list and answer the following questions for each.

1. What about this organization interests you?

2. Why do you think this organization is important to your community?

3. In what ways has God equipped you to participate in this movement?

4. How could you participate in this organization in order to learn more?

CONCLUSION

We never cease to be amazed by what God can and will teach us if we will just listen. It doesn't matter if we are the Avoider, the Wounded, the Helper, or the Observer. The important thing is that we claim our present reality and learn from it. We must not run from it but toward it and toward the transformation that God wants to enact through our listening, asking, being, and doing. And we must not do it alone but with a group of people with whom we can journey on this dangerous road that takes us deep into the heart of God.

BENEDICTION

Now, may the God of presence and the God of the present reveal to you who you are in him. May you be challenged to ask yourself the tough questions. May you allow others to speak truth into your life. May you practice being his and then acting out of his resources. And may you continue to place your life inside his story!

When you were a child, what fictional character or non-fictional person was your hero? Why did you look up to this character or person?

What do you think about the Jürgen Moltmann quote on living in the present? Where would you say you spend the majority of your time living (past, present, or future)? Why?

To which of the four characters in the story do you most relate at this time or in a particular situation? Why?

How might you embrace where you are on the journey? What might it look like to be transformed into Christ's image at this particular point in your journey?

What do you see as the difference between being and doing? Toward which are you more likely to lean?

What is one thing you could do to be the person God wants you to be in our world?

Have you ever been tempted to give up on the Church? Why?

Discuss some of the projects you worked on in this chapter. How did God transform you through them? How did they help you better understand the story, yourself, others, and the world around you?

Chapter Four

WHO IS MY NEIGHBOR?

WOVEN TOGETHER: A CABLE COMMUNITY

A metal chain provides us with a good understanding of how our world views community. We are a bunch of individual links, each with our own strengths and gifts, which come together to form a bond. But there are a couple problems with metal chains. First is that the strength of the chain is dependent upon each independent link; it is only as strong as its weakest link. Second, each link is connected to only two other links—one to the left and one to the right. So when the chain is pulling a heavy load, the connection points are actually pulling against each other, placing all the pressure on each individual link to keep itself connected to the others. It's no wonder, then, that our world favors this model of community: this model only enhances the tendency in our society to value the individual.

Maybe a more accurate metaphor for healthy community is the steel cable. Unlike the chain, the steel cable consists of a bunch of individual strands of wire that are woven together like a braided rope. The larger the cable, the more layers it has. For instance, a giant cable designed to hold up a bridge might consist of ten large cables that have been woven together. Each of these large cables is made of ten medium cables that have been woven together out of ten smaller cables that each consist of ten individual strands of wire. The strength of the cable lies in the fact that each wire is not connected at just a few points but rather throughout the entire surface length. Therefore, the tension is spread out evenly over the whole surface. If a few individual strands break, the cable doesn't immediately fall apart. Instead, the weight is redistributed over the remaining strands.

Living out this picture of community is a lot more intimidating than the metal chain model. Creating a greater bond between individual "strands" requires more vulnerability. Our strength as a community exists in the reality that we are all sharing the load in one way or another. As a result, less stress is placed on any one person or on any one group. This model allows the community to bear the load when its members are going through difficult times and remains strong when some choose to walk away. The community finds even greater strength when it unites with other communities that share the same vision; thus, we can more positively speak of collaborations between other churches and other denominations and sometimes even other organizations that don't share the same faith system.

So how does this model of community help us understand and define "neighbor?" For most of us this word denotes location. Our neighbor is the one who lives in the house next door, the apartment below us, or who works in the cubicle beside us. In this context, like the metal chain, neighbor refers to the links on either side of us. We may not even like our neighbor but because we share something—a yard, a fence, or a wall—we create a loose bond and try to work together when we have to.

But what if we shifted our way of thinking around the steel cable model? Jesus' understanding of neighbor requires greater connection and accountability to those around us. Part of the strength of the "cable community" is our ability as a Christ-centered community to be intimately tied together, bound by Christ's love and our ability to welcome others into this community at whatever place they find themselves in the journey. Being a neighbor, therefore, means extending the community's strength and love to everyone who comes across our path.

THE JEWISH UNDERSTANDING OF NEIGHBOR

The question of what it means to be a neighbor is at the heart of the parable of the Good Samaritan. Yet, in order for us to understand what is being asked by the expert in the law and answered by Jesus, we must place our passage back in its context. In Luke 10:27 the lawyer quotes Leviticus 19:18 ("love your neighbor as yourself") as part of his summation of the law, and consequently as part of his understanding of what it means to remain a part of God's covenant people. But his understanding of neighbor is tied up in his understanding of Leviticus 19:17-18 in its context. There we read:

"Do not hate your brother in your heart. Rebuke your neighbor frankly so you will not share in his guilt. Do not seek revenge or bear a grudge against one of your people, but love your neighbor as yourself. I am the LORD."

The words "your brother" and "your people" make it clear that the expert understood "neighbor" to refer to other Jews, and more particularly, to other Jews who had remained faithful to the covenant God. In fact, the Hebrew word translated as "neighbor" in verse 18 is often translated as "friend." This definition reinforces the expert's understanding of neighbor as someone with whom a person normally associates. And for the law-observing Jew, this specifically meant other law-observing Jews. Part of this understanding is no doubt linked to the Jews' very difficult geographic and cultural context. They were a uniquely God-called people often surrounded by others who wanted to kill them and take their land. They were also a people very susceptible to idolatry and assimilation with other religions. This is why God closely guarded their purity (see Deuteronomy 7:1-5).

Their understanding of neighbor didn't mean Jews treated others badly. Leviticus 19 has much to say about how one is to treat the "alien," or foreigner (see especially verses 9 and 10 and 33 and 34). However, what it does mean is that many, like the expert in our story, had come to justify purity over people as part of their commitment to God. Jesus' parable strongly calls this misguided commitment into question.

JEWISH/SAMARITAN RELATIONS

In this context, to say that Jews and Samaritans were not good neighbors is a grave understatement. Though geographically adjacent, they were anything but neighborly! The beginning of the Samaritan people is much debated, but 2 Kings 17 attributes their existence to the importation of inhabitants from Babylon, Cuthah, Avva, Hamath and Sepharvaim into Samaria by the Assyrian king who had conquered the Northern Kingdom. These new inhabitants adopted the worship of Israel's God while still holding on to their native gods. For this reason, the Jews viewed the Samaritans as unclean and spoke of them with great contempt. They said things like: "Even while these people were worshiping the LORD, they were serving their idols. To this day their children and grandchildren continue to do as their fathers did" (2 Kings 17:41). Tensions no doubt rose between these two groups when the Jews were trying to rebuild the Temple in Jerusalem. The Samaritans wanted to help, but the Jews refused them, saying, "'You have no part with us in building a temple to our God'" (Ezra 4:3). Thus, the Samaritans did everything in their power to frustrate the Jews and slow down the building of the Temple. Later, they even tried to stop them from building a wall around Jerusalem (see Nehemiah 4:1-4).

In the New Testament, we see the result of years of tension. By this time the Samaritans had built their own temple of worship on Mount Gerizim (see John 4:20) and the rift between these groups was so great that most Jews avoided Samaria and Samaritans altogether. This is why the Samaritan woman Jesus spoke with in John 4 was so surprised when he asked her for a drink of water (v. 9). In Luke 9:51-55 we see the disciples ready to rage against the Samaritans when they refuse Jesus lodging on his way to Jerusalem. Probably the most offensive reference to Samaritans in the New Testament takes place in John 8:48, in which Jesus is accused of being a Samaritan and demon-possessed. In this exchange, we can see clearly what the Jews thought of the Samaritans. They linked them with demons and believed them to be incapable of speaking the truth or of understanding the truth of Scripture.

JESUS' UNDERSTANDING OF NEIGHBOR

With this brief history we can now see how offensive Jesus' parable of the "good" Samaritan would have been. Jesus makes the "bad" Samaritan the hero and the "good" Levite and priest the villains. When we get to the end of our parable and Jesus asks the lawyer who the true neighbor had been in the story, the lawyer can't even bring himself to say "Samaritan," opting instead to say "the one who had mercy on him." Jesus had reinterpreted Leviticus 19:18 and the Jewish definition of neighbor. No longer did it refer to friends or family. No longer did it refer to only the Jews. It now meant something completely different. Neighbor now referred to all of humanity, and the covenant people of God were those who exemplified God's compassion and love in tangible ways to everyone in their path. The apostle Paul said it this way:

> You are all sons of God through faith in Christ Jesus, for all of you who were baptized into Christ have clothed yourselves with Christ. There is neither Jew nor Greek, slave nor free, male nor female, for you are all one in Christ Jesus. If you belong to Christ, then you are Abraham's seed, and heirs according to the promise. (Galatians 3:26-29)

Through the faithfulness of Christ and our union with him, we have come to represent a covenant people who no longer value worldly categories. However, these categories—Jew or Gentile, slave or free, male or female, rich or poor, black or white, insider or outsider, Christian or non-Christian—have created distance rather than unity and have provided us the justifications for ignoring our neighbors and withholding love from those whom God brings across our paths.

There is profound truth and freedom in the reality that no matter our differences and distinctions, we have all been created by the same God. This God provides salvation for all people (see John 3:16; Titus 2:11); is actively pursuing every lost sheep (see Luke 19:10); and uses his body, the Church, to reach the world for him (see Romans 10:14-15). For this very reason, we are called to be neighborly to everyone we meet. We are to love people with his love so that they too might come to know, understand, love, and worship the creator God—for in loving others, we are loving him (see Matthew 25:31-46).

Questions

What is the strongest, healthiest community of which you have ever been a part? Does (or did) this community look more like the chain link model or the steel cable model?

What does it mean to "justify purity over people?"

What groups in our world share a similar contentious relationship like the Jews and Samaritans?

How does your relationship with Christ change your view of what it means to be a neighbor?

COMMUNITY MEMBER

Think about a community of which you are a part. It could be your neighborhood, church, school, book club, a class at your gym, and so on. Interview a member of the community to come to an understanding of the importance of the steel cable image of community. Here are some examples of questions:

1. How long have you been a part of this community?

2. How did you come to belong to this community?

3. In what ways have you received strength and support from your relationships in this community?

4. In what ways have you given encouragement and support to others in the community?

5. In what ways do you feel isolated from the community?

73

A MODERN-DAY PARABLE OF NEIGHBOR

Jane was not unlike most teenage girls: she fought with her parents, had a messy room, sent and received far too many text messages, and had a relatively low self-esteem. She grew up going to church with her family, and there was a time when she knew God, even felt close to him. But as she grew older, she wandered from God. At sixteen, Jane's life changed dramatically when she found out she was pregnant. Her parents were understandably shocked and saddened by this news, but they were also compassionate. They encouraged her to keep the baby and told her she could continue to live with them. They assured her they would do everything they could to help her bring her child up in a loving home.

In the early months of Jane's pregnancy, life remained relatively unchanged. However, as the weeks passed and she could no longer hide the baby growing inside her, she began to feel the pierce of judging eyes all around her. Some of Jane's closest friends seemed to abandon her in her time of greatest need. In fact, Bridget and Carrie, good friends from church with whom she had grown up, started avoiding her at school.

One day when Jane was eating lunch alone, she was approached by Amala. Amala was a quiet girl with very few friends. Many people ridiculed her because she was different. Amala was born in Iran but had moved to the States when she was still a baby. She and her family were devout Muslims. In fact, Amala wore a hijab (a scarf that covered her head and neck), which made her stand out at school. She was no stranger to the feelings that Jane was now experiencing. Maybe this was why Amala approached Jane that day. Maybe this was why the two of them connected so quickly and found friendship in a very unlikely place.

Five years later, Jane and Amala are still friends. Because of her friendship with Amala, Jane named her daughter Hope. Amala, whose name means "hope" in Arabic, showed Jane kindness when others didn't. Her friendship reminded Jane that she was not alone. Actually, it was Amala who helped Jane return to the relationship with Christ she had once had. No, Amala has not become a Christian. In fact, Amala continues to be very committed to her own faith, but this important difference has not stopped the two of them from being close friends.

Who is the best neighbor you have ever known?

From your perspective, what does it mean to be a good neighbor?

Has someone ever been a better neighbor than you expected him or her to be?

Who are the most neighborly people in your church?

How can we be loving neighbors to those whose faith differs from ours?

Questions

RETELLING THE PARABLE

Take the opportunity to create your own narrative of the Good Samaritan story. What is the story's setting? Who is the person in the perilous situation? Who are the people who should help but don't? Who is the outsider who comes to the rescue? How does this situation end?

Project

A TRUE STORY OF NEIGHBORS

On October 2, 2006, in a small town outside of Lancaster, Pennsylvania, a tragic event unfolded at the West Nickel Mines Amish School. The day started off normally, as a couple dozen children ages six to thirteen and a few teachers gathered into the small one-room Amish school with its quaint school bell on the roof and its fenced-off schoolyard nestled in the peaceful landscape of rural Pennsylvania. But this peace was soon shattered when thirty-two-year-old Charles Carl Roberts IV entered the school armed with many weapons. Roberts ordered the boys and all the adults to leave the school and then bound the ten remaining little girls and barricaded the doors. Police arrived soon, but before any negotiations could take place, Roberts shot off several rounds. When the police finally broke through the barricades, they found a horrific scene. Roberts had shot himself but not before shooting all ten girls. Three girls died immediately, two others died in the hospital the next day, and one remains in a wheelchair to this day.

Questions of why quickly rose to the forefront of the investigation, and some possible answers did surface. It appears that Roberts was seeking revenge on God, either for the death of his own daughter some ten years earlier or for some other unknown incident that had taken place twenty years earlier. Whatever the cause, Roberts left his wife, three of his own children, and a whole community in shock and anguish. But while many of us watched the story on television and angrily questioned why this happened or what could be done to prevent it from happening again, those most intimately affected took a more gracious approach.

This Amish community did the unthinkable. Instead of being angry, the families and community of those who had lost their children responded with love. Instead of revenge they showed compassion. Instead of pointing fingers, they forgave. They didn't just say the words; they lived out grace. The community quickly rallied around the killer's family and expressed their sadness for their loss and grief. They prayed for the family, sent cards and gifts, and many even attended Charles Roberts' funeral. Many who observed this grace unfold were bewildered, angry. They asked, "How can they forgive this evil man?" Some people even judged this community for their lack of anger at this grave injustice that had taken place. But this small Amish community paid little attention to what the world around them was saying. Instead, they lived out and continue to live out the grace and strength they received from God.

How do you think you would react if something similar happened to you? How would your faith in Christ aid and challenge you?

Respond to this quote from the book *Amish Grace: How Forgiveness Transcended Tragedy.*

> In a world where faith often justifies and magnifies revenge, and in a nation where some Christians use scripture to fuel retaliation, the Amish response was indeed a surprise. Regardless of the details of the Nickel Mines story, one message rings clear: religion was used not to justify rage and revenge but to inspire goodness, forgiveness, and grace.[1]

Why do you think we get angry when others don't react as we think we would?

What is the greatest example of forgiveness you have ever received? What is the greatest example of forgiveness you have given?

Questions

RADICAL GRACE

Have you ever witnessed an example of un-fathomable forgiveness and grace? If one does not come to mind, Google a story of radical grace from the recent past. What happened in the situation that created the need for forgiveness? Who offered the act of grace? To whom did they offer it? How was the gift of forgiveness received? What happened to their relationship following the attempt at reconciliation? How does this story challenge and change you?

Project

CAN I BE A NEIGHBOR?

> "You have heard that it was said, 'Love your neighbor and hate your enemy.' But I tell you: Love your enemies and pray for those who persecute you, that you may be sons of your Father in heaven. He causes his sun to rise on the evil and the good, and sends rain on the righteous and the unrighteous. If you love those who love you, what reward will you get? Are not even the tax collectors doing that? And if you greet only your brothers, what are you doing more than others? Do not even pagans do that? Be perfect, therefore, as your heavenly Father is perfect." (Matthew 5:43-48)

Like the Parable of the Good Samaritan, these words from Jesus strike hard against our natural instinct as sinful human beings. We have a hard enough time loving the people we call friends and family. How is it possible for us to love the "other" or the enemy? Each of us has created a caste system of relationship (whether consciously or unconsciously) in which we justify treating some better than others. Even as Christians, we defend our right to love the believer and hate the sinner. We might not say it aloud or use these exact words, but our actions reveal our hearts. While Scripture does talk about caring for the body of believers, it also talks about doing everything we can to bring others into this body.

Indifference is not an option for followers of Christ. We have come face to face with a new reality—one that contradicts the world around us. We are now kingdom people and as such, we live by a new set of rules. These rules are not based on humanity's limited understanding or on humanity's attempt to create harmony through power and war. The rules of the kingdom are grounded in relationship—first in our relationship with God but then also in our relationship with others. Yet as we have already seen, the line between these two is blurred in Scripture to the extent that loving others is loving God. This kind of love does not originate from us but from God. In other words, when we love others with God's love (taking our own motivations and desires out of the equation), we are truly loving God.

This is why loving *all* of our "neighbors"—family, friends, the "other," and enemies—is so liberating. But we can't do it in our own strength. In order to love people the way God calls us to, even those we want to love, we must rely on his Holy Spirit to work in and through us. Therefore, loving others is not so much about learning to put up with attitudes or idiosyncrasies in others that annoy us or even about finding common ground; it is about learning to allow the love of God to flow through us. It is about being transformed from the inside out so we begin to see people not from our perspective but from God's! For this reason, loving our neighbors is not an option. It is first and foremost part of who we are and then, and only then, part of what we do.

Have you ever thought that loving people is liberating? Why or why not?

React to this quote: "Each of us has created a caste system of relationship (whether consciously or unconsciously) in which we justify treating some better than others."

Can you name a time when you experienced a specific act of love from someone you considered an enemy?

Have you ever sensed that God was offering love "through" you? What was that like?

Questions

LOVE THY ENEMIES

Make a list of all the enemies you have had in your life. Why do you view these people as your enemies? What would it mean to love them? What specific action could you take to show them that you love them? Write out a brief prayer that you think God would want you to pray concerning this person.

Project

CONCLUSION

In this chapter we have tried to look at "neighbor" from a variety of perspectives in order to come to a clearer understanding of what Jesus meant when he used the word. We have sought to wrestle with difficult questions that challenge what we do but also challenge who we are in Christ. If we continue to think of the concept of what it means to be a neighbor in our own narrow and subjective constructs of location, of friend, and of doing, we will have missed the joy of being a neighbor, which is wrapped up in the joy of belonging to Christ.

BENEDICTION

Now, may the neighborly God, the one who loved you even though you were his enemy and even though you persecuted him, make you a vessel of neighborliness from whence he might flow. May he be allowed the freedom to transform you from the inside out so he might transform others through you. And may you find great joy in this often slow and difficult process.

What is your definition of neighbor? How did you arrive at this definition?

How do the images of the chain link and the steel cable help you understand and examine life in a community?

What practices have you experienced that help build strong relationships in a community?

What categories (race, gender, religion) do people use to separate people in your city or town?

What categories do you find that create the most distance for you and your relationships?

Discuss some of the projects you worked on in this chapter. How did God transform you through them? How did they help you better understand the story, yourself, others, and the world around you?

Chapter Five

DEFINING DISTANCE

CONQUERING DISTANCE

Distance is relative. A few hundred years ago, most people couldn't fathom venturing beyond the earth: the moon and planets in the night sky must have seemed like another realm of existence. But in our day, we have not only been to the moon: we left our flag there and have now moved on to make our mark on more distant celestial locations. In the past hundred years, the same can be said for our exploration of the deep caverns of the ocean or the internal chambers of the human body. The vast distances that were once sources of great mystery are now within our reach.

In the same way, in the mid-1800s it would have taken months to travel from Boston to Kansas City by carriage. When families moved west along the Oregon Trail, they went with the realization that they would most likely never return to their hometowns, their extended families, their friends. A century later, in the mid-1900s, travelers who owned an automobile or who could afford train tickets could move between these two cities in a number of days. In the late twentieth century, affordable air travel made it possible for many Americans to cross the U.S. in only a few hours. Today, through the mass ownership of mobile phones, the explosion of social media, and the almost universal access to the Internet, a person in Boston and a person in Kansas City can connect by phone, e-mail, instant messages, or video—all with the click of a mouse. Our technology has made the world an incredibly small place.

But despite our ability to conquer almost any distance, the question remains: have we really moved any closer to one another? From the comfort of our couches, we use our smartphones to access almost any image or learn almost any piece of information by simply entering a few words into a search engine. We may spend a vacation in a foreign land, even visiting famous landmarks, but we don't really know what it is like to live there on a daily basis. We may visit a friend on the other side of the world, but despite our ability to sample the native food and try the regional clothing on for size, we may never know what it is to live in their shoes. And the emotional distance we create even with those with whom we share a home can make them strangers to us and us to them.

This is all part of the mystery of distance: we can grow so close so quickly, but a distance always remains. In the story of the Good Samaritan, the literal distance we have to wrestle with is simply the distance of walking from one side of a dirt road to the other. But whether we cross that skinny road relates to another distance—a distance that is not always so easy to recognize and is even more difficult to cross.

CREATING DISTANCE

Imagine you are walking along a main street in your town or city. What people or things fill the sidewalk? What storefronts do you pass? Now, imagine you look ahead. As you take note of the people who are in your path, what types of people or specific people would cause you to cross over to the other side of the street? What about them makes you want to create distance? Are you afraid they'll physically harm you? Are you afraid of what they might ask of you?

For example, a recent parolee may dodge a police officer in order to avoid a possible altercation. A young mother might avoid a suspicious-looking man sitting on a city bench. While some distancing may be necessary, when we continually concern ourselves only with our own safety, we risk failing to see others at all. Instead, we view people as obstacles we must move around, avoid, or step over on our way to our intended destinations.

This is the situation in the Good Samaritan story that Jesus tells. The text makes it clear that the priest and Levite see the man in need from far enough away that they are able to pass by on the other side of the road. In Chapter 4 we discussed how the priest and Levite in the story are culturally closer to the man who is robbed than is the Samaritan. One of the great ironies of the story is that the two people in the story who share the most culturally with the victim are the ones who neglect him most blatantly. It reminds us that throughout history, living in close proximity with someone or even sharing similar characteristics does not necessitate that two individuals or groups will treat each other as neighbors.

To where outside of your state or country have you traveled? Describe your experience relating to the people and cultures.

What was the best or healthiest neighborhood you have ever experienced? What made it such a positive experience for you?

Who are the people who live closest to you? Would they consider you a neighbor? Why?

What would treating someone like a neighbor look like? Have you ever lived in a community where this was the case?

Questions

MAPPING YOUR WORLD

Where you live is as important as where you don't live. Think about your town. What different cultural groups (ethnic, social, generational, and economic) exist in your area of residence?

In the journal section of this chapter, draw a simple map of your town. Then, ask yourself the following questions.

1. Where do the people in these groups live?

2. Where do the members of these groups shop? Go to school?

3. Does a physical separation (if one exists) cause these groups to avoid one another?

4. What does it mean to avoid certain people?

5. What people do you avoid by where you live, shop, eat, go to school, or go to church?

6. How does the practice of avoiding people create an unspoken distance between you and them?

NEIGHBORLY ATROCITIES

On July 15 and 16 in 1942, the police of Paris, France, rounded up 13,000 of their Jewish neighbors and handed them over to Hitler's Nazi regime. The vast majority of these 13,000 people, including children, who were eventually physically separated from their parents by the French police and transported to Auschwitz, were sent to concentration camps and murdered. This event, known as the Vel d'Hiv roundup, depicts the great failure of humans to treat their neighbors as neighbors. It is one of many extreme examples of the distance that can exist between peoples, whether they are separated by culture, ethnicity, or religion.

When we hear a story like this one we find ourselves overwhelmed with questions. How could an event like this happen? How could someone get to the place where they are willing to sacrifice their own neighbors, including children? How can people who live so close together be separated by such a distance that they would inflict atrocities upon them? While these are important questions, which need to be addressed, we find ourselves wondering what can be learned from these atrocities. Most people look back on their own 'shady' past and either beat themselves up, deny it, or justify it. For years this was the case with France, but in more recent years, they have provided us with a different picture—one from which we can learn.

In 1995, the sitting French President Jacques Chirac spoke about the Vel d'Hiv roundup in a national address and attempted to accept responsibility for the government and citizens that allowed such horrific events to take place during that World War II period. In his speech, Chirac admitted that "France, homeland of the Enlightenment and of human rights, land of welcome and asylum; France, on that very day, accomplished the irreparable . . . Failing her promise, she delivered those she was to protect to their murderers."[1]

· · ·

In the movie *The Sandlot*, James Earl Jones plays an old man who lives in a house near the baseball field where the neighborhood boys play together. James Earl Jones's character, Mr. Mertle, owns a dog that the boys believe has a history of killing children. The boys live in fear of this man whom none of them has ever met and a dog they know only through a fence. However, by the end of the film, the dog and the old man become the children's friends, and they realize the man is not only kind but also passionately shares their love of baseball.

Whether factual or fictional, horrific or mundane, there are examples all around us of how ignorance and misunderstanding can quickly create tensions between two groups of people. In fact, anywhere distance exists between groups, we tend to fill that distance with distrust and make-believe, creating myths in place of what we don't know for sure. And the most frightening truth is this: we will always find whatever we're looking for. The Vel d'Hiv roundup is an extreme, but not unparalleled, example of what can happen if that distance is not named and dealt with appropriately.

Every day we create distances of varying degrees between ourselves and others, opening the door to potentially volatile situations between ourselves and those we should instead love and respect as neighbors.

Have you ever lived in a neighborhood in which you felt like people who lived near you were your enemies?

How could people who live so close to you be seen as your enemies? Reflect on conflicts from a more recent era (e.g. Hutus and Tutsis in Rwanda; Serbs and Croats in Yugoslavia).

Of what people in your community are others jealous?

About which people in your community do people make up myths?

A RELIGIOUS EXPERIENCE

Martin Luther King, Jr. once described Sundays at 11 a.m. as the most segregated hour in America.[2] The goal of this project is to challenge you to decrease the distance between you and someone or some group you have avoided in the past.

With a group of friends, attend a religious meeting of an ethnic group different from your own. Ask yourself or each other these questions about your experience.

1. What is the atmosphere like when you enter the house of worship?

2. When and where does this group meet?

3. Does this group own their building?

4. Who leads the gathering?

5. Is there music?

6. How does the entire experience compare with your typical Sunday?

THE NEED TO CREATE DISTANCE

In John 17, Jesus offers a prayer for his disciples, both present and future. This passage could serve as a catalyst for discussion on a number of topics, but concerning distance, two specific proximities seem to be on Jesus' mind in this chapter. The first is the distance between the Son and the Father. In verses six through ten, Jesus states that he has revealed the Father, his glory, and his words to those who have received him. In fact, his prayer is that the closeness of these followers would be like the oneness of the Father and the Son. There seems to be a sense that despite the physical separation of the Son and the Father, they share a closeness that makes them inseparable. Jesus then prays that his followers may be one as he and the Father are one (see verse 11). Jesus seems to be praying that his followers would learn to live in the unity that he and the Father share—a unity that transcends any distance.

The second distance is the one between the followers of Jesus and the world. Twice in verses fourteen through sixteen, Jesus states that his followers are not of the world as he is not of the world. But in verse eighteen he declares that these followers have been sent into the world on mission—just as he was sent into the world. According to Jesus' prayer, this mission revolves around our living in such unity that the world becomes aware of the love of God at work in and through us (verses 20-23).

The Church's mission, then, is to be present in the world but have an identity that comes from the world's creator. So in some way the fact that we have the ability to be in close proximity to some people, events, and circumstances while remaining separate is actually positive. It is simply part of the ability to be not entirely objective, but transcendent. As Christian theologian Miroslav Volf writes:

> Christians are not the insiders who have taken flight to a new "Christian culture" and become outsiders to their own culture; rather when they have responded to the call of the Gospel they have stepped, as it were, with one foot outside their own culture while with the other remaining firmly planted in it. They are distant, and yet they belong.[3]

Volf challenges us to see that being a Christian does not mean we are divorced from the cultures in which we live. It means that we live simultaneously in two cultures—the culture of the world and the culture of God's kingdom come in Christ. In living out our new lives as Christians, there are times when we must make decisions that challenge the worldviews that are widely accepted around us. We do this because our allegiance and identity come from another place. In this way, as Volf has stated, "we are distant and yet we belong."

It is important to remember that there are times when maintaining or creating distance is necessary in order to remain healthy and safe. Abandonment can be a responsible reaction to certain situations. For example, alcoholics need to distance themselves from establishments where alcohol is served. Children who leave a violent home may need to live in a safe environment away from the dangerous influence of their birth families. Young adults who grow up with negative influences may want a new start at college or work, far away from their former hometown. People who have experienced a negative expression of religion may need to find a church body that can serve as a place of healing, restoration, and inspiration. Whatever the scenario, it is vital for us to be able to recognize when creating distance is actually the necessary step for creating a healthy and obedient lifestyle.

In the Parable of the Good Samaritan, we believe that Jesus was suggesting that the Jews needed to abandon certain ideologies about God and power. Thus, when the Samaritan engages the beaten man, he is crossing more than just a street. While he is closing the distance to the man in need, he is simultaneously creating a distance between himself and something else. In this particular case, Jesus is suggesting that the Samaritan is abandoning the cultural ideology that shaped so much of the relationship between Jews and Samaritans. As Volf suggests, "at the very core of Christian identity lies an all-encompassing change of loyalty, from a given culture with its gods to the God of all cultures."[4] The

Samaritan is abandoning the idea that this Jewish citizen in need is his enemy and instead is embracing him as a neighbor to be loved.

The Samaritan in our story is Jesus' example of the ability to love your neighbor as you love yourself. But here Jesus is pushing the limits of the cultural boundaries that would have kept others from helping this person in desperate need. This ability to transcend one's culture is what is missing in the priest and Levite and is most expressive in the Samaritan. In distancing themselves from their own neighbor who is in need, the priest and the Levite are unable to abandon the laws of purity even when these laws are in conflict with the law of love. But the Samaritan, in serving this person who is not his religious or ethnic equivalent, abandons the cultural ideologies that would keep him from loving his neighbor as himself.

Who or what do we need to abandon for our own good?

What prejudices and practices of your culture need to be avoided?

From what habits, places, and people do we need to distance ourselves?

Have you ever avoided helping someone because you feared that doing so would make you "impure?"

Questions

Project

BRIDGING THE DISTANCE

Take time to visit a shopping center or restaurant in your city that is culturally distant from your own. Then reflect on the following questions.

Shopping Center

1. What does it feel like to enter that space?

2. What items are sold that are different from the ones in the stores where you normally shop?

3. Is literature or media sold there? If so, how does it differ from your own experience?

Restaurant

1. What is the atmosphere like?

2. How do the menu items differ from what you are used to ordering?

3. How does the food taste?

4. Take notice of the people around you. Are they families or singles?

CONCLUSION

Distance matters. Distance influences how we live every day. But it is important in a world where we can so easily overcome distances that were once insurmountable that we recognize there are still some distances with which we have difficulty dealing. Like the distance between you and that relative who you need to ask to forgive you. Like the distance between you and the bad habit you have been trying to break.

In the same way, the physical distance in our story is only a few steps, yet this distance seemed impossible to the priest and the Levite, who were too self-focused to aid their fellow citizen. Still, that same physical distance for the Samaritan, one which should have seemed like crossing the Atlantic, was simply a matter of placing one foot in front of the other until he had left the old ideology of exclusion and entered into a new world of embrace.

BENEDICTION

May the God who himself crossed an infinite distance to make himself known to us empower you to cross the distances you need to this day in order to extend his love more fully in and through you.

Are we able to make a distinction between distances that are necessary and those that are detrimental?

From what things do you need to distance yourself (e.g., assumptions, perceptions, racial/cultural ideologies)?

Have you ever felt that despite how physically close you are to someone, you still have a large distance between you and that person? How did this make you feel? What did you do to try to close up that distance?

Have you ever felt like people were avoiding you? Why do you think that might be? How did being avoided make you feel?

What is the most difficult distance
that you have ever tried to cross?

What is the greatest distance
that you think exists between the
Church and the world?

Discuss some of the projects you
worked on in this chapter. How did
God transform you through them?
How did they help you better
understand the story, yourself, others, and the world around you?

Chapter Six

MODERN-DAY SAMARITANS

RAZING WALLS

Walls have many practical and beneficial uses. Their primary purpose, though, is to *hold in* or *keep out* someone or something. They can provide protection and define boundaries. But the very fact that we believe we need to be protected means we perceive that we live in a dangerous world. The fact that we have to define boundaries means that we have reason to separate ourselves from others. We live in a broken world where fear and distance define us. Wouldn't it be nice to live in a world where we didn't need to build walls to protect us or to keep undesirable people out? It is difficult for us to imagine a world like this. We prize our privacy to such an extent that the idea of having *no* walls may sound more intimidating than having *too many* walls. But maybe this is because most of us have never lived in captivity.

November 9, 1989 marked the official fall of the Berlin Wall in Germany. On this day, travel restrictions for East Germans were lifted and many of the borders were opened. That night, many East Germans crossed the wall and experienced West Germany, and freedom, for the first time in twenty-eight years. And while the physical wall took years to build and years to tear down, the emotional wall of separation was much more flimsy and easily destroyed. This statement is evidenced in the East German citizens' growing unrest and protest against the communist government that held them captive, their thousands of attempts (some successful, others fatal) to escape by any means possible, and their quick reunification with Western Germany. It seems then, that this wall had not truly been constructed in their hearts and minds.

Walls are not always made of brick and mortar or wood and drywall. Sometimes walls are built with words we use to shield us from others or to push others away. Sometimes our walls are built through our actions. In fact, body language can raise many walls. Sometimes we even construct walls in our mind that don't actually exist, physically or otherwise. Yet, for those who have erected the walls and for those who have perceived the walls, they are as real, as tangible, as concrete or cinder block.

So how can we begin to raze the walls we have constructed? Maybe the first question is how we can arrive at a place in our lives where we no longer want to build walls. Some of these topics were addressed in the last chapter on distance, but here we must grapple with some very real walls that have been constructed by us and by our world—walls that must be torn down. In Chapter 4 we looked at the very real barriers that separated the Jew and the Samaritan. While most of us are removed from this rift, we wrestle with our own modern-day Samaritans. They are those who are not like us, and for this reason we marginalize, even persecute, them. Now we must move toward seeing—and then toward loving—them.

THE OTHER

"Sticks and stones may break my bones but words will never hurt me." So goes the saying, but we all know this isn't the case. Words are some of the first weapons we wield. As children these weapons begin in the form of name-calling, which doesn't stop when we reach adulthood. Instead, the weapons become more sophisticated and the ways we employ them more camouflaged. Although we adapt our weapons as we age and mature, their purposes remain the same: we want to hurt, to control, to separate. That's what name-calling is. It is a way for us to place people in categories so we can keep them at arm's length. The reasons are also the same. We are ignorant and afraid! We fear those who are different from us, those we don't understand. We fear the "other."

In the pages that follow, we explore five broad categories in which much of our ignorance and fear of others occur. We are purposely using the titled categories of economic, ethnic, political, religious, and sexual rather than the more derogatory labels that our world employs. Labels such as rich or poor, legal or illegal, Democrat or Republican, Christian or Muslim, gay or straight all focus on what we are or what we think the other is. Attaching these labels and those like them to others often begins as innocent classification attempts but quickly leads to mean-spirited name-calling. When we label people, we often reduce them to whatever label we attach to them. As a result, they lose their humanity, becoming only "*that*

Democrat" or "*those* Muslims" with whom we disagree. Instead, we need to start seeing who we are and who the other person is from God's perspective. Only once we move past objectification will we be able to move toward reconciliation, relationship, and being a neighbor.

ECONOMICALLY OTHER: HEARING THE OTHER'S STORY

Through making generalizations and giving credence to stereotypes, we avoid intimacy. We label others as rich or poor, place them into a category with a preset story, judge them accordingly, and then justify why we should avoid them at all costs. We look at the woman driving down the road in her expensive, imported car, and we assume she is privileged or an elitist (more labels) who has never worked a day in her life and who probably spends all of her time and money gratifying her own selfish desires. We look at the homeless man on the corner begging for money and assume he is lazy and that he got where he is because he is a drug addict, an alcoholic, or a deadbeat husband and father (still more labels).

If we would only try talking to each other, we might learn that the homeless man was an accountant who is down on his luck and is doing whatever it takes to feed his wife and three children. Or we might learn that the woman is a molecular biologist who not only works very hard for her money but is also developing a cure for breast cancer. We never know who the person is until we get to know who the person is! Sounds obvious enough, but are we willing to take the time and energy it will take for us to hear the other's story?

More than any of the other Gospels, the Gospel according to Luke focuses on Jesus' ministry to the poor, the outcast, and the marginalized. For this reason, it has a lot to say about our current category. There are many statements that seem to favor the poor over the wealthy: Jesus' mother, Mary, celebrates the God who has lifted up the humble and filled the hungry while humbling the rulers and sending the rich away empty (1:52-53); John the Baptist says those who have much should give to those who have little and for those in power to be just to those under them (3:10-14). Jesus quotes Isaiah 61:1-2, saying he has come to preach the good news to the poor, freedom to the prisoner, sight for the blind, and release for the oppressed (Luke 4:18-19; 7:22-23); he calls the poor blessed and says the rich have already received their reward (6:20, 24); and he tells the rich young ruler to sell everything he has and give it to the poor (18:22). Yet, this gospel doesn't condemn the rich. Instead, we learn that Jesus often kept company with the rich (5:29; 19:2-5); ministered to and sought the salvation of the rich (7:1-10; 19:1-10); traveled with and was supported by many wealthy women (8:2-3); and taught stewardship of one's wealth (16:1-12; 19:11-27).

Thus, we learn that the labels of "rich" or "poor" should not define the person. Rather, we must learn to look past what a person has or doesn't have to see who the person is on the inside. The rich and poor alike are called to use their resources for the kingdom. In order to truly be the body of Christ, we must look past our economic differences and learn to work together. If we spend our time and energy passing judgment, we will not love well, and if we don't love well, we will not represent Christ well.

When you see the economically other,
what assumptions come to your mind?

Why do you think we pass judgment on
people who are different from us?

How can we cross the distance to the
economically other?

In what ways do you regularly interact with
those who are economically other than
you? Is your goal of the relationship to
change them?

EYES WIDE OPEN

Read through these staggering facts and statistics about poverty in our world: 22,000 children die each day due to poverty; 1.1 billion people lack access to clean water; nearly 1 out of every 2 children in the world live in poverty. Even more overwhelming for us are some of the statistics on how much the world spends on frivolous items compared to what it would cost to solve some of the world's poverty issues. For instance, the U.S. spends $8 billion a year on cosmetics and yet we could provide education for all children in the world for $6 billion a year. Europe spends $11 billion a year on ice cream, but for only $9 billion a year we could provide clean water and sanitation for all.[1]

To read more go to: http://www.globalissues.org/article/26. What stands out to you the most? What feelings did you experience as you read through this report? Why do you think this is? Tell someone else something you learned and start a dialogue about poverty and our role in being part of the solution.

ETHNICALLY OTHER: DISCOVERING OUR ALLEGIANCE

Ethnicity, nationality, and race are difficult subjects for us to talk about since so many people's primary self-identification is determined by these markers. For this very reason they divide us more than any other. *I'm American. I'm Asian. I'm Caucasian. I'm Russian. I'm African. I'm Latino. I'm Indian.* The list goes on and on. While it certainly isn't bad to be proud of one's heritage or of one's country, as Christians our relationship with Christ supersedes all other identity markers. This also means the laws that dictate our relationship with Christ supersede all others.

For example, if you are married and you are also a member of a sports team, you know that each of these relationships has laws and bylaws, whether clearly stated or not. One would hope that the priority of your marriage would supersede that of the sports team. Therefore, your first commitment would be to your spouse, and any allegiance to or requirement of the sports team that would harm your marriage would have to be refused—even if it meant being removed from the team. Therefore, if you are _____ (fill in your nationality here) and a Christian, you must know where your primary allegiance stands. If your country or government requires you to do something that jeopardizes your relationship with Christ, what should you do?

Also, no matter how Christian we believe our respective nations to be, we cannot fall into the trap of combining our nationality with our faith. Christianity is not about religion: it is about relationships! Even if the entire population of a country had a relationship with Christ, that country would still not be Christian because a country, a government, or a location cannot be in a relationship with Christ.

So what does all this mean? It means that as Christians we must move past our hate and our judgment of those who are ethnically different from us. As Christians, we recognize that all of humanity has been created by God and therefore we all share a common image (see Genesis 1:26-27). We cannot be racist because we are all part of the human race. We cannot hate our brother or sister because we share a common Father. How might we embrace our similarities rather than focusing on our differences? Leviticus 19:33-34 states:

> "When an alien lives with you in your land, do not mistreat him. The alien living with you must be treated as one of your native-born. Love him as yourself, for you were aliens in Egypt. I am the LORD your God."

These words remind us of what we have in common. They push us to raze the walls of division and embrace the other as our own. They force us to remember God's grace toward us and seek for this grace to be realized in the other. They force us to love!

In what ways do we tend to combine our nationality with our Christianity? What do you think about these practices?

Take some time to evaluate your primary allegiances. What are they? Where does your allegiance to Christ fit?

Questions

Do your actions (where you spend your time and money and how you treat others) reveal anything about your true allegiances? What?

TRACING YOUR ROOTS

Trace your ancestral roots. This activity may take some work on your part. Start by talking to your family, of course: parents, grandparents, and extended family members can be great resources. Try to trace back at least to when your family first came to the country in which you now reside. Try to find out why your ancestors left their native country or countries and why they chose the country in which you now live (if this is even the case for you and your family). It would also be nice to try to discover how your family was treated when they arrived in this new land.

All of these questions may take some additional searching on the Internet in order to get a general idea of the history. Once you have as much information as you can find, reflect on what you have learned.

POLITICALLY OTHER: LEARNING TO DISAGREE WELL

Politics is one of those subjects that can break up a good party in seconds. It seems some live and breathe politics and others avoid any engagement with the topic like the plague. When we think of politics, our minds normally jump to government, parties (Republican, Democrat, and so on), and politicians. Yet the most elementary understanding of politics is the process by which two or more people make a decision. Most of us live by a set of principles or beliefs that we believe are important for a healthy life, community, and world. If our convictions run deep, these principles may be worth fighting for—and maybe even worth dying for. This is why we must learn to enter into dialogue about some of the underlying ethical and moral principles that undergird our strong convictions. If we spend all of our time and energy debating the individual issues, we will likely never agree on much, but if we begin to understand the guiding ethics and morals of a particular person or group, we might learn to argue less and seek to work together more.

In the Church there is often a naïve belief that we should all share the same convictions when it comes to political issues. We are surprised to learn that other Christians disagree with us on the issues about which we are so passionate and adamant, especially if our moral and ethical convictions are grounded in Scripture. We are, therefore, often quick to pass judgment, labeling someone un-Christian or unbiblical for the stance he or she holds. Yet, what we fail to realize is that those with whom we disagree might also be basing their convictions out of their understanding of the Scriptures.

What would happen if we started to dialogue about each other's underlying moral and ethical convictions—not in an attempt to prove the other person wrong but rather in an attempt to understand how they arrived at their viewpoints? As followers of Christ, we should be committed more to each other than to a particular political party. We will not always agree, but we must learn to disagree in more loving ways—not by ignoring the conversations but rather by seeking to find commonality in our shared devotion to Christ.

Read and engage with these words by Shane Claiborne:

> As I continue to wrestle with complex human and political issues, I resolved myself to one thing: the starting point must be that the church is a place where we can grapple with difficult questions with grace and humility. And I believe that, even more important than thinking identically on every issue, we must learn to disagree well. Our ability as a church to disagree well is as powerful a witness to the larger society as our uniformity on every issue.[2]

Are you a political junkie or a political
avoider? Why do you think this is?

Do you think all Christians should agree on
certain political issues? Which ones? Why
these and not others?

Respond to the Shane Claiborne quote
about learning to disagree well. Do you
agree or disagree with his statement?
Why?

Questions

Project

POLITICAL ISSUES

Sit down and make a list of political (social, financial, global) issues that are important to you. Be as specific and extensive as possible. If you need to, Google "political issues" and you will find plenty. Now, try to see if you can trace the moral and ethical foundations behind your convictions (e.g. justice, freedom, caring for family, compassion, and so on). Do you see any patterns? Do you see any inconsistencies? Do you always act out of your convictions, or do you sometimes act out of convenience?

RELIGIOUSLY OTHER: FINDING COMMONALITIES

It is a sad reality that Christianity is divided and splintered by seemingly innumerable denominations. It is even more disheartening to see many of these denominations fighting one another as if they are competitors. When we speak about unity but tear down rather than encourage and join with others who share very similar doctrinal and theological precepts, we drown out our own voices. More importantly, we often validate our non-Christian critics—the ones who rightly believe we are unloving hypocrites. What if our world is waiting for the Church to engage it with fewer words and more action?

Beyond that, when we engage those of other religions, we're often far less kind than we are to other Christians. Members of all religious groups have, at one time or another, spoken ugly words to and about those of different faiths. It should come as no surprise, then, that our world is becoming increasingly secular and that people are turning to social services, government, and non-faith-based non-profits for help and direction. And why shouldn't they when we're all too busy fighting with each other to help those who need us? So how might we begin to find commonalities rather than differences?

At their core, most religions teach a desire to help those in need and to promote justice and love. While we can all point to times when each of the major religions has not lived out these principles, pointing fingers at each other will not change our world. We must stop passing judgment on those who are different from us. We don't have to accept all the teachings or beliefs of the other, but we must begin to bridge the gap that divides us. Our Christian faith requires us to love the other in spite of their religion—or lack of religion. The Good Samaritan in our story was not Jewish in his faith, but that didn't stop him from reaching out in love.

Too often we have been like the prophet Jonah: God wants to use us to bring a message of repentance, salvation, and hope to the religiously other, but we refuse. Not because we are scared of them hurting us but because we are scared of them actually accepting God's message and repenting. We have already judged them as unworthy, and therefore we can't fathom them being deserving of God's grace. Like Jonah, we sit under a tree and whine, and like Jonah, we need to hear God speak:

> But the LORD said, "You have been concerned about this vine, though you did not tend it or make it grow. It sprang up overnight and died overnight. But Nineveh has more than a hundred and twenty thousand people who cannot tell their right hand from their left, and many cattle as well. Should I not be concerned about that great city?" (Jonah 4:10-11)

We must seek to find commonality in our shared desire to see the world transformed and in the reality that we are all created by God. We must seek to love and reach out and recognize that we never know how God might use our faithfulness to transform lives for him.

How have you passed judgment on people of other faiths? Why do you think you did this?

Take time to read the Jonah story. Do you relate to Jonah? How?

Do you think the world has given up on the Church? On religion? What might we do to change their perceptions of us?

In what ways can we work with other religious groups?

Project

A DIFFERENT PERSPECTIVE

Take some time to do a little research about another religion. If you can find a copy of their sacred text/s, read a few chapters. After you have done your research, reflect on the following questions: How is this religion different from your own? How is it similar? How does your learning about this group change your perspective? How does it start to break down walls of fear?

SEXUALLY OTHER: LOVING WELL

From as early as the first three chapters of the first book of the Bible, we quickly see that the relationship between man and woman is not going to be a simple one. In Genesis 1:26-27 we learn that all humanity, both male and female, was created in God's image and likeness and given authority over God's creation. In Genesis 2:18-24 we learn that men and women were created to complement each other and to become united as one. Then in Genesis 3 all hell breaks loose (literally). In the span of just a few verses, humanity falls to sin, passes blame, hides from God, is cursed, and then is kicked out of the Garden of Eden. Talk about a bad day!

If we were to continue on through Genesis 11, we would see an ever-widening gap within humanity and between humanity and God. Sin has affected us at our core, and we are foolish to think we can change without God's grace. For this reason, we shouldn't be amazed that there are constant disagreements between the two genders. We shouldn't be shocked to see men trying to control women or women trying to manipulate men. We shouldn't be astonished at the objectification of humanity. We shouldn't be stunned by the overall perversion of the God-given gifts of love and sex. We shouldn't be startled by the choices we see in relationships, whether they be gay, straight, bisexual, or other. We shouldn't be taken aback because we have read the story and have seen firsthand the impact of the fall and the results of sin in our world.

What *should* surprise us more than anything is the way Christians treat others (and even each other). If Christ teaches anything, he teaches his followers to love well. If Scripture teaches anything, it teaches us about grace and forgiveness. We should be experts at living out grace, forgiveness, and love because we have experienced these things in life-changing ways. Listen to these words from Paul:

> Therefore, if anyone is in Christ, he is a new creation; the old has gone, the new has come! All this is from God, who reconciled us to himself through Christ and gave us the ministry of reconciliation: that God was reconciling the world to him-

self in Christ, not counting men's sins against them. And he has committed to us the message of reconciliation. We are therefore Christ's ambassadors, as though God were making his appeal through us. We implore you on Christ's behalf: Be reconciled to God. (2 Corinthians 5:17-20)

Therefore, we must be ambassadors of reconciliation to our world, not counting their sins against them, but sharing the transforming love of God with them. We must leave the judgment to God because he has left the loving to us. Some might say we are called to love well in spite of our differences; we would say we are called to love well *because* of our differences.

Where are some places in the church where gender issues have caused division?

Have you ever thought of yourself as an ambassador of reconciliation? What does this phrase mean to you? How would it look played out in your own life?

React to this quote: "It is one thing to be *against homosexuality*, to affirm that the Bible rejects the practice of same-sex lifestyles, but it is another to be *against homosexuals*, to let your disagreement with their behavior spill out in your feelings and words toward them as people. It is unChristian to lose your sense that everyone's fallen nature affects all aspects of his or her life, including sexuality, and to forget God's command to love people in order to point them to Jesus."[3]

HEARING THE OTHER

Interview someone you consider sexually other than yourself (in gender or self-identification) in order to understand their perception of how they are viewed by the Church and by the culture around them.

1. What experiences with religious organizations have made them feel their sexual identity is celebrated, accepted, or diminished?

2. What experiences with the larger culture around them have made them feel their sexual identity is celebrated, accepted, or diminished?

CONCLUSION

This has been a difficult chapter. We have addressed many of the walls our society, and we ourselves, have erected. We have sought to understand the implications of allowing these walls to stand and have tried to challenge you to find ways to raze these walls in the places where you find yourself. Like the Good Samaritan, we need to practice seeing; we must learn to see the needs of those around us. The only way this is going to happen is if are willing to move out of our comfort zones and hear the other's story.

BENEDICTION

May the God who shows no partiality teach you to do the same. May you discover the freedom in razing walls of division and building bridges of commonality. May you choose to reach out to those who are different from you, and in so doing, may you find that we are not that different after all.

What are some labels that have been placed on you? How did these labels make you feel?

Name and discuss some additional categories of "other" (e.g., generationally other).

Which of the categories mentioned in the chapter were most challenging for you? Why?

Which of the categories do you think is most challenging for the Church as a whole? Why?

Can you think of other walls of division that have been constructed or razed in our world?

Discuss some of the projects you worked on in this chapter. How did God transform you through them? How did they help you better understand the story, yourself, others, and the world around you?

Chapter Seven

EXTENDING THE CIRCLE
OF CONCERN

ADOPTED

Do you know anyone who was adopted? In recent years, adoption has received increased attention, thanks to famous adoptive parents like Angelina Jolie and Sandra Bullock. In fact, a number of famous people were adopted. Have you ever been to Wendy's for a hamburger? The founder, Dave Thomas, was adopted. Have you ever listened to the Beatles? John Lennon was adopted. Have you ever used an iPod? Steve Jobs, founder of Apple, was adopted into his family as well. Adoption is actually more prevalent in the U.S. than any country in the world.

Adoption practices have morphed over the centuries. Historically, the Hebrews did not have a formal practice of adoption. There were provisions within the Law for the community to care for the orphan, but this practice looked more like kinship care rather than any social system of adoption we might recognize. Their tight communal and familial bonds, as well as their living conditions, allowed for a more natural inclusion of orphans into societal life. In New Testament times, when the areas around the Middle East were much more complex ethnically and politically, there was a provision within the overseeing Roman society for orphans to be adopted into families.

According to Roman law, adopted children lost all connection to their former heritage and were officially recognized as children of equal status to birth children in their new families. All debts the children might have carried from their former families were canceled and the children became equal heirs of their new father's inheritance. Being adopted meant they were on equal setting with birth children: there was no differentiation. This was an especially important legal policy for those families who were concerned about carrying on their political line because they lacked a biological heir. Many of the emperors of both Jesus' and Paul's day actually received their royal status through adoption.

This political and social reality is particularly evident in Paul's letters. For Paul, the image of adoption is an important metaphor for understanding the relationship God has offered humanity as a result of Christ's redemptive action. In Galatians 4:4-7 he writes:

> But when the time had fully come, God sent his Son, born of a woman, born under law, to redeem those under law, that we might receive the full rights of sons. Because you are sons, God sent the Spirit of his Son into our hearts, the Spirit who calls out, "*Abba*, Father." So you are no longer a slave, but a son; and since you are a son, God has made you also an heir.

Think of the many images often associated with God in our society. If you were to do a quick Google search, you would see numerous images of the Almighty in the form of a senior adult on human growth hormones posing on a cloud with a thunderbolt in hand. But Paul wants us to understand a different picture—the image of a loving father, an *Abba*, who could be trusted. For Paul, Jesus' invitation is not to a new religion or *polis*, but to a new family.

Paul continues his use of adoption language in Romans 8:14-17:

> . . . those who are led by the Spirit of God are sons of God. For you did not receive a spirit that makes you a slave again to fear, but you received the Spirit of sonship. And by him we cry, "*Abba*, Father." The Spirit himself testifies with our spirit that we are God's children. Now if we are children, then we are heirs—heirs of God and co-heirs with Christ, if indeed we share in his sufferings in order that we may also share in his glory.

Here, Paul uses the image of adoption to describe how God has taken those who were far off and brought them close to him. Three themes run through both of these texts in regards to adoption. First, there is a new identity; these people are no longer slaves but children. Second, this new identity is seen in the empowerment of the Holy Spirit. Finally, there is a new reality whereby these children now stand to receive the benefits of full inheritance. For Paul, adoption is the image by which those who were once considered outsiders can now understand themselves as accepted, full members with Christ in their Father's family.

FAMILY RESEMBLANCE

When children go through an adoption process, one of the primary concerns for all of the family members involved is how they will fit into their new family. Will the adopted child get along with his or her new siblings? Will he or she stand out at school or in public when people see the child next to family members? In families formed by birth, we can usually look at other members of our family and see similarities in our physical features. This can also be true in families formed by adoption. Over time, our similar life patterns cause us to take on the physical traits of our family. And whether we are part of families formed by birth or by adoption, we all tend to take on the personalities and tendencies of the families of which we are a part. This recognition of family traits is an important part of our ability to discover the ways we are connected to others. In a greater sense this is not limited to our nuclear families.

In Matthew 25:31-46, Jesus tells the Parable of the Sheep and the Goats. This passage describes a day of future judgment in which people are separated based on their actions. The Son of Man acts as a shepherd, separating the goats out of the flock in order to set aside his sheep. The passage describes how the shepherd makes the distinction between the sheep and the goats. The sheep are those who have been faithful in caring for their shepherd when he was in need, whether hungry, imprisoned, or sick. The goats, on the other hand, have not been faithful in their concern for him and are therefore dismissed.

One of the most interesting aspects of this passage is the level of surprise that exists not only in those who are judged to have been unfaithful but also in those who are judged to have been worthy. The sheep are aware that they have been living out the compassion and care their Lord expected of them, but they were unaware that their care for "the least of these" was actually care for the Lord. The great irony is that even those who have been called faithful did not recognize that the people they were serving were not just strangers but family members of the king. Jesus' words in verse 40 are that "'whatever you did for one of the least of these brothers of mine, you did for me.'"

We also see this dynamic at work in the story of the Good Samaritan. The Levite and the priest pass by this beaten man even though they may recognize him as being ethnically similar to themselves. But the Samaritan looks past the cultural and ethnic difference to see a person in need, a person worthy of his time, attention, and care. While the Samaritan may see the wounded man as a Jewish enemy, he also recognizes him as a neighbor, or a family member, in need. At that moment, he adopts him into his family—and loves him.

This is the lesson of the Parable of the Sheep and the Goats that we see lived out in the Good Samaritan. Even though we may see the differences that exist between us relationally, ethnically, and biologically, we must also, as fellow members of God's family, learn to recognize that we are all part of the family of God.

What adoption stories have you recently
seen in the news?

What resemblances do you share with
members of your family?

How has adoption intersected with your
own life?

How does the idea of adoption relate to
your own experience of faith?

Have you ever recognized Jesus in
someone else?

Questions

Project

GROUP RESEMBLANCE

Think about a group of which you are a part. It may be your family unit, your church, or a group of friends. The key is that you have belonged to this group for an extended period of time. What likenesses do you share with these people? In what ways have you come to "resemble" others in this group? This could be through habits you have, ways you dress, speak, or think. How has being a part of this group influenced who you have become?

WHAT IF IT WERE YOUR SON?

In the movie *John Q*, Denzel Washington plays John, a father whose son has been diagnosed with a potentially fatal heart condition. The boy's only hope is an impossibly expensive heart transplant that John's health insurance will not cover and his limited income cannot possibly afford. In a climactic phone call from the hospital where their son is receiving care, John's wife reveals to him that the health insurance will not cover any further hospital stays—which means their terminally-ill son is about to be released and sent home. She pleads with him to do something. So John, a normally upstanding citizen, takes an entire emergency wing hostage in a desperate attempt to get his son the life-saving transplant he needs.

Imagine your child were about to be denied the medical treatment that was his only hope of survival. What would you do to ensure he received the treatment? Or what if your parent needed a new kidney? Would you go door to door until you found a donor? What if your children didn't have a safe school environment? Would you attend the school board meetings until something changed? What if your children went to sleep hungry every night? Would you steal to make sure your family did not starve? These scenarios don't just happen in the movies; families face dilemmas like them every day. And these are the questions we must wrestle with as we engage Jesus' vision for the rest of the world.

How would our lives change if we began to look at everyone in need as a member of our own family? What would we risk if we began to see everyone as someone who God has invited to be a part of his new family?

THE CIRCLES THAT SURROUND US

While conceptualizing everyone in the world as being part of the same family is certainly a lovely thought, living out this idea is an entirely different challenge. None of us can be best friends with everyone. While those who live in small towns may in fact know everyone they encounter on a daily basis, the same cannot be said for those who live in urban settings. City dwellers cannot possibly meaningfully engage everyone with whom they come in contact—which is why they are sometimes thought to be cold or rude. However, the reality is that creating distance and maintaining anonymity are vital skills when living in such close proximity to so many people. This is certainly the case with Jesus and his ministry. Jesus had thousands of onlookers and hundreds of followers, but an inner circle of only twelve disciples. And within the inner circle, there were those who seemed to be chosen for an even more intimate experience. If you don't believe this, just try to name the twelve disciples. The ones you can remember were probably part of Jesus' inner circle.

As you reflect on the world of relationships that surround you, imagine your world as a ripple of relationships where there are people who are closer to you and people who are further away. Imagine the relationships in your life as a target with concentric circles extending from the inside to the outside. You are the bull's-eye. From the center moving out, there are naturally those who are in closest relationship to you. This first ring includes the people who are most like you. These may include your family and closest friends: your spouse, children, siblings, and maybe even a few college roommates. These are people with whom you have shared intimate moments. They are the people you would call in the middle of the night to come to your rescue. They are the people who support you when life is difficult.

But this circle also includes the broader group of people who are like you. These may be people for whom you naturally have an affinity, the people you would willingly be seen speaking to in public. For instance, when you use public transportation or are in large public gatherings, these are the people toward which you naturally gravitate. This circle might include people who are of the same ethnicity, age, or gender as you. They are the people you would "see" if they were in need or in trouble. This is your circle of immediate concern. To borrow from Jesus' parable in Matthew 25, if these people were hungry, thirsty, or naked, you would not only notice; you would take action.

Moving out from the inner circle to the next circle, we see those who are the "other." These people differ from you in ethnicity, age, gender, or religion. In public places, you do not naturally remain close to them. They may make you uncomfortable because you have had little contact with them, and, thus, do not know them. Maybe they have a different sexual orientation or political position from you. Maybe they dress radically different from you or live in a part of town that you don't frequent. Whatever the differences, these people make up the "other." This circle is filled with people to whom you may not naturally lend anything or for whom you would not go out of your way. If they had a need, you probably would not hear about it firsthand, and therefore would not naturally go out of your way to help. Most likely, you are not in a close enough relationship to ever know when they are in need.

This final category is the outer ring of the circle. This circle is far beyond your friends and family and even past those you consider neutrally "other." These are your enemies—ones who you probably know more fully than those who are simply "other" but for whom your level of contempt places them at the greatest distance. In this circle are those who, from your perspective, stand against you. They may be literal enemies in a political sense, or you may simply despise their perspective and ideology. This circle may include people who have harmed you in the past or continue to harm you. They are the people we try to keep out of sight and out of mind. These circles of concern remind us that there are reasons why we avoid certain people; there are reasons why we wouldn't clothe, feed, or visit certain people.

The challenge of putting people in this final outer circle is that if we are really going to call ourselves followers of Jesus, we cannot allow them to stay there forever. Consider the example of the Good Samaritan. He could have easily passed by this man, considering him an enemy, and no one would have blamed him. In fact, those hearing this story for the first time likely would have *assumed* that the Samaritan would treat this enemy as an enemy. But if we consider ourselves part of Jesus' family, is having enemies an option?

If we are part of Jesus' family, don't we have to learn to embrace all those whom he has invited to be part of his family as well?

Who are the people in the circle closest to you?

Think of three people you interacted with today who are the "other" in your circles.

Think of three people you consider enemies. What makes them your enemies?

When was the last time you recognized Jesus in the face of someone in need?

Questions

"TARGETED" PRAYER

Using a page from your journal, draw four concentric circles to form a target. In the center of the target, write your name. In the circle that surrounds your name, write the names of friends and family members who come to mind. In the next circle, write the names of people you engage daily but with whom you don't have much interaction. Next, think about the people who are "other" from you and write down their names. In the final circle, reflect on those you consider your enemies. Now, use the list to pray for people in each of the circles. Which people can you pray for most easily? Which are the most difficult? What do you pray for them? What do you think God would want you to pray for them?

> "When you reap the harvest of your land, do not reap to the very edges of your field or gather the gleanings of your harvest. Do not go over your vineyard a second time or pick up the grapes that have fallen. Leave them for the poor and the alien. I am the LORD your God." (Leviticus 19:9-10)

In this passage we see God's desire for his people to not only care for those closest to them but also to find ways to expand their circles of concern to include the poor and the alien. Leviticus 19 was about including people in small ways within the security and stability of the greater society. By following God's command to leave food for those who would otherwise go hungry, the Israelites would care for and influence those around them.

Later on in Leviticus 19, the author reminds the Israelites that they must care for aliens and the poor and include them in their circle of concern because that is what God did for them when they were foreigners in Egypt. And if Israel's story is our story, this same command must also affect us. For us, this passage is a call to open up margins in our lives to include those closest to us, the other, and even our enemies—because we were once foreigners in God's land. We were once strangers and even enemies, but now we are family. We cannot forget the grace and mercy that God has shown us; instead, we must continue to extend this same grace and mercy to others.

Imagine what our world would look like if instead of returning evil with evil, we repaid evil with good. This is the challenge of Leviticus 19—that we would not only take care of the poor, the widow, and the orphan, but that we would also extend graciousness to those who are enemies in our land. God's hope for us is that we will continue (or begin) to incorporate those who exist on the periphery of our circles. To do so, though, we must expand our circles of concern and choose to no longer operate in such a way that we keep an eye out only for those we value, those who can do something for us, those for whom we feel a sense of responsibility.

Through this text, God is challenging the limited circles of concern out of which we live.

Now look back at our imaginary circle of concern. Where is Jesus located? We often assume Jesus is standing next to us in the center, but what if Jesus is standing on the outer perimeter calling us to move toward him? Too often, we act as if following Jesus requires us to simply take care of those who are closest to us: then, if there is any energy or resources left, we can toss the leftovers to the outer circles. Jesus makes it clear that we can all love our brothers and sisters; we can all love the people who do things for us and show us love. But to really follow Jesus is to find concrete ways to love those on the farthest reaches of our circles of concern.

How can you open up margins in your life
to include others?

Have you ever felt that you were on the
outside looking in?

What practices in our society are similar to
those in Leviticus 19?

Why do you think we have a tendency to
keep people out of our inner circle?

Questions

EXTENDING YOUR CIRCLE

Take a look at the circles that you created in the last project. Now take a name from each of the three circles that you have created: families and friends, the other, and the enemy. After each of these three names, write a concrete action that you will try this week in order to express your desire to include them as a member of your family circle.

CONCLUSION

Jesus is trying to remind us that the boundary lines we have a tendency to draw in the world are not big enough to claim membership in his family. If we move to extend our circles of concern to include all of humanity, all God's children, strangers and friends, then the reality is we can't live desperately for all of them. We can't avail ourselves to be everybody's solution. But while it is impossible to be everything for everyone, it is important that we be something for someone. It is important that we extend our circle of concern to a new "family member" somewhere, somehow.

BENEDICTION

May God awaken you this day to how you can extend the circles of your own concern. May God use you to embrace those who may not recognize themselves as God's family. May our *Abba* use you as a vehicle of his ever-extending embrace this day.

Discuss some movies you've seen in which a character or characters extend their circle of concern.

What does it mean for you to view God as Father?

What "family resemblances" do members of your church community share?

Have you ever been desperate to do something for a family member in need? What was that experience like?

Have you ever felt like someone was reaching out in order to include you into his or her circle of concern? How did it make you feel?

Have you ever had a hard time accepting someone as a part of Jesus' family? Why?

Discuss some of the projects you worked on in this chapter. How did God transform you through them? How did they help you better understand the story, yourself, others, and the world around you?

Chapter Eight

SERVING THE "OTHER"

YOU ARE WHO YOU EAT WITH

Most of us have childhood memories of going to a restaurant or a relative's house for a special meal. Maybe you celebrated Christmas at your grandparents' house or birthday parties at your favorite restaurant. These celebrations can be incredibly treasured moments that mark the most precious occasions of our lives. Think back to a holiday you celebrated with extended family: you can probably remember a special dish or dessert that marked the occasion. But even more important than the food (we hope) was the company with whom you shared the meal.

Many of us eat lunch in a public setting. Whether it is a school cafeteria or an office lunchroom, who we eat with is part of our social status, our public persona. College lunchrooms as well as office spaces often have a code of identity tied to who we eat with. While the old adage "you are what you eat" may be true, it is often equally assumed that "you are who you eat with." In a real way, our table fellowship is representative of who we are. In Jesus' time this was no different: social and religious status determined who people were willing to sit with at a table (take a look at Peter's concerns in Acts 11). Jesus himself is criticized for the table company he keeps. He jeopardizes his status as a Jewish teacher and prophet when he chooses to sit down for meals with the wrong crowd—tax collectors and sinners, for example.

In John 13 we see a very important meal taking place. Jesus has made preparations to celebrate the Jewish Passover with his closest friends. This meal is the annual celebration of God's deliverance of the Israelites from slavery in Egypt thousands of years before. It is also a type of hopeful optimism that God will send another deliverer in the future. Jesus' followers have come to believe that he might be the mighty king that has been sent to overpower their enemies. But his followers are about to experience a great letdown when he allows himself to be captured, tortured, and killed in the coming hours. In those hours the disciples display their disappointment and fear, as many succumb to the pressure to abandon, deny, and betray him.

153

Nevertheless, during this meal, Jesus, who is well aware of their expectations, offers a foreshadowing of the kind of king he desires to be. As the disciples enter the room, it would be customary for a person of low status to be there to clean the dust from their feet, but Jesus takes the place of the servant and washes them himself. Later on in the evening, Jesus, who is the host of this special celebration, breaks bread and pours wine, offering them both to his friends. His humility is again on display when we realize he offers this meal, this bread and wine, symbols of his body and blood, to these disciples even though they are the ones who will betray, abandon, and deny him.

We too are called to serve those who are not only different from us, but who we might consider our enemies. This is something that Jesus not only speaks about but literally does in the celebration of this meal. As we see, he offers the cup to Judas, the one who will betray him. He offers this meal to Peter, the one who will deny him. The failure of others to live up to his expectations is not a deterrent to his offer of relationship. He does not deny a place at the table even to those he knows will soon abandon him.

In Chapter 7 we discussed how we can begin to extend our circle of concern to those we are called to recognize as family members. But how can we do so in concrete ways? Jesus served meals. The Samaritan lent a hand. What can we do?

HOSPITALITY IS THE NEW EVANGELISM

In her book *Making Room: Recovering Hospitality as a Christian Tradition*, theologian Christine Pohl renews a vision for understanding the significant role that hospitality plays in the mission of the Church. According to Pohl, our welcoming of others in the Church and into our lives is more than politeness. Rather, "our hospitality reflects and anticipates God's welcome."[1] In the preface to *Making Room*, Pohl describes how during her twenty years of experience in the ministry of hospitality, she often recognized that there were those who went unseen in our society and that this invisibility was a detriment to not only the individual but to the greater community as well.

For Pohl the practice of hospitality is an act of the recognition of others as equals and image bearers of God's likeness. She suggests that hospitality must include both the ability to see every human being as one's neighbor and also to engage the stranger personally.[2] Pohl's work is a challenge for the Church to take up the task of hospitality not simply as an invitation to our own lives, but even more as an invitation into the story of God that we share together. When we practice biblical hospitality, we embrace people as family and not simply as objects from which something can be gained.

This hospitality is seen in many practices, but it is probably most associated with an invitation to a meal. This meal can be shared at a private table in one's home or a corporate communion table in the sanctuary, but in either case it can carry on the important work of the invitation to the kingdom life of Jesus. As they were in the New Testament, meals become a symbol of the breaking down of social barriers in the new reality of Jesus' followers. The Jesus meal is not an invitation to charity, which is too often about *my* generosity; rather, it is an invitation to Christ's compassion and a real attempt to share life as neighbors with the other and the enemy.

Who is the best host you know? What makes him or her a great host?

What do you think you would have done if Jesus had asked to wash your feet?

What would it look like to show biblical hospital as Jesus did?

When was the last time you were invited to a meal at another person's house?

When was the last time you invited someone to a meal at your home?

Questions

PRACTICING HOSPITALITY

In order to practice hospitality, take an opportunity to invite someone over for a meal. Be certain to take this opportunity to listen to the other person. Practicing hospitality means creating a space in which another person can see that you are offering to be a neighbor to them.

Project

LOVING THE "OTHER" WITHIN OUR WALLS

As we discussed in previous chapters, being in close proximity to others does not mean we will share a close level of intimacy with them. In fact, there is a danger in our churches that we will become separated from other groups that exist even within our own walls, especially with the generationally other. Over the past few decades there has been a tendency to categorize our worship gatherings by the personal preference of worship styles. This is usually done by separating groups based on music styles, theological perspectives, or cultural differences. But remember that being the church is about unity rather than uniformity. It is important that despite our differences, we learn to live and love together. Doing so is our witness to a watching world.

One particular church that we know of is actively serving the elderly in their church who are not able to be physically present during Sunday corporate worship gatherings. This church creates a list of those who are shut in and gathers a team that on a Sunday morning travels to the homes of these members. The congregants then spend time visiting, praying, and sharing communion. It is a way of reaching across to the generationally other and letting them know that if they are unable to make it to the community, the community will be brought to them. In doing so, they are attempting to show the elderly that they are still a valuable part of the community.

The need to offer hospitality within the walls of the church is not limited to the generationally other. In fact, there are serious renovations going on concerning how we embody our global mission within the church around the world. Not long ago, a group of college students went on a mission trip to serve in an area that was culturally other than their own. The interesting aspect of this trip was that these students did not bring any building materials or prepare to do a Vacation Bible School program. Instead, this group simply spent a week listening to their brothers and sisters from another culture speak about their experiences.

What if our mission trips were not just about helping but about healing the distances that exist in our churches? Too often the Western Church travels to faraway places with good intentions and resources, thinking their greatest need is our financial or physical help. But oftentimes, we hear about people who return from a mission trip having discovered they gained more than they gave.

There is a grassroots movement in the Church to form global partnerships between local churches in different world areas. This is an attempt to move past the idea that certain areas are more equipped to bring the gospel to other areas. Instead, those who are part of this movement recognize that churches all over the world have the opportunity and responsibility to carry out the mission of the Church. Financial resources are exchanged, but the real exchange takes place as pastors and people from both cultures and areas of the Church sit, eat, listen, and share.

For example, a partnership exists between a church in Boston and one in a southern section of Guatemala City. The people of the Guatemala City church have recently suffered under years of natural disasters. From a Western perspective, this congregation in the global South is in an uphill battle and lacks the financial resources to enact real change for themselves and their community. They are working to transform a neighborhood that lacks proper education, clean water, safety, and infrastructure, and they are doing so with no paid staff and very few financial resources.

But Pastor Jose and his Guatemala City congregation are incredibly resourceful. By working with a water filtration company, they are now able to offer purified water to their community. In addition, they have created a music program for kids in which they teach them a skill that gives them a way to express themselves. They are also creating an educational institute for adults who desire to improve their possibilities of finding work. Finally, they are working to establish micro loans as a means to enable their neighbors to move out of poverty. So while the church in the North is offering some material resources to their neighbors in the South, the real hope for this partnership is in a mutual exchange of friendship and support. Through this beautiful partnership, both churches are learning how to close the distance between the members of their global family.

There are endless redemptive stories like this taking place all over the world every day—ways we are learning to be our brothers' and sisters' keepers as God has called us to be.

What groups do you consider "other" even
within your own church?

Why do you think there is distance
between groups at your church?

What person or people in your church are
attempting to cross these distances?

Have you ever traveled on a mission trip?
What did you give? What did you gain?

Questions

COMMUNITY BELONGING

Identify three groups within your church that you might consider the "other." Think about why these groups might feel they are the "other" within your community. Choose one of these groups and talk to your pastor or church leader about your concerns. Ask if there is a way you might participate in bringing the community to this group.

LOVING THE "OTHER" OUTSIDE OUR WALLS

On March 24, 2011, a new musical by the creators of *South Park*, a cartoon on Comedy Central, opened on Broadway. While the musical's producers, Matt Stone and Trey Parker, are certainly not strangers to controversy, especially regarding their irreverent use of religious material, few people could have imagined that they would create a full-length Broadway satire on a single religious group. But that's just what they've done with *The Book of Mormon*, a spoof on Mormonism.

Considering the circumstances, the Church of Jesus Christ of Latter-Day Saints (LDS) handled the situation remarkably well. Before the show's opening, they merely issued a statement that said, "The production may attempt to entertain audiences for an evening, but the Book of Mormon as a volume of scripture will change people's lives forever."[3] The LDS did not take this opportunity to create a public outcry as a means of protecting their own reputation. Instead, with class, dignity, and grace, they responded to a group that has mocked them to audiences of millions in the past and whom many would view as their enemies.

Just as significant to the story, though, is the response of the producers of the show. After hearing the statement from the LDS, the creators of *South Park* and the musical simply said, "Every time we do something Mormon, their response makes us like them more."[4] In this instance, the LDS modeled hospitality to a group that lies outside the walls of their own identity and life.

In Chapter 3, we talked about Jeremiah 29 and how the Jewish people were anticipating deliverance from their exile. God had a different plan for them, though: his people, who were living within the walls of their enemies, were to use this time as an opportunity to move outside the walls of their own concern. God's message was "don't just worry about yourselves." For so long, they had thought that being God's people was about them receiving things from God. In this less than encouraging word from God, he said, "'Seek the peace and prosperity of the city to which I have carried you into exile. Pray to the LORD for it, because if it prospers, you too will prosper'" (Jeremiah 29:7). God was saying, "If you really want peace, it will require change on your behalf. If life continues to be about your best interest, then nothing will ever change, but if you seek the good of your enemy, you will change the world."

It is important to remember that the peace that God is speaking of is not simply the absence of conflict. It is the *shalom* of the Hebrew Scriptures—God's dream for the world. But shalom will not come from simply waiting quietly and keeping one's distance. It comes only through engaging the "other" and one's enemies. Shalom also transforms the way we pray, moving us away from asking God to change the world so that we get what we want to asking God to change us so that the world gets what it needs. We become a people who are aware that life is no longer about us and what we want and only assuring that our desires are met. Shalom is a kind of peace rarely seen in the world, but when it is present, it can bring radical transformation and remind us that God's future is still on its way.

In the years following apartheid in South Africa, there was still great strife and hostility between the once-ruling ethnic minority and the now-ruling ethnic majority. If the new leadership had come into power simply with the intention of repaying wrongs, it would have fractured this already-fragile nation. It was during this time that the forward-thinking governing bodies created a number of actions that were meant to create an atmosphere of forgiveness. The following is a quote from Desmond Tutu regarding how to treat the "other" and the enemy even when they have mistreated you. He says:

> In forgiving, people are not being asked to forget. On the contrary, it is important to remember, so that we should not let such atrocities happen again. Forgiveness does not mean condoning what has been done. It means taking what happened seriously and not minimizing it; drawing out the sting in the memory that threatens to poison our entire existence. It involves trying to understand the perpetrators and so have empathy, to try to

stand in their shoes and appreciate the sort of pressures and influences that might have conditioned them.[5]

In the story of the Good Samaritan, we see the Samaritan show this kind of empathy in his willingness to place himself in the same hazardous situation as the beaten man. In the same way, forgiveness displays what it means to place oneself in the position of the other in order that love may be extended across any roads or boundaries that may separate them.

Does your church have "enemies?" How have these people come to be seen as such?

Read Jeremiah 29:1-14. What do you think of the often-quoted verse Jeremiah 29:11 after reading the whole passage?

Has anyone ever shown you compassion even when he or she didn't have to?

Have you ever washed someone's feet or had someone wash yours? If yes, what was that experience like? If no, what do you think it might be like?

CONCRETE EXPRESSION OF LOVE

Think about who might be considered an
enemy of your church. Identify three groups
that you think might fit into that category.
Choose one group and talk to your pastor
or small group leader about why you think
your church might view this certain group
as an enemy. Think of a way you might offer
a concrete expression of love to this group
as a church.

Project

CONCLUSION

In John 21, Jesus invites his disciples, those who have been his betrayers, deniers, and abandoners, to eat breakfast on the beach. As Jesus approaches them on the beach, they do not recognize him, but he prepares a meal for them. As the breakfast ends, Jesus strikes up a conversation with Peter. Peter has been guilty of denying Jesus multiple times, but Jesus does not use this meal as an opportunity to punish or scorn Peter. Instead, Jesus utilizes this breakfast as an opportunity for restoration. In these moments of hospitality, Jesus invites Peter to renew his call.

Jesus knew how to live out hospitality. His life was an invitation to God's kingdom come and coming again. Jesus' table fellowship was an image of how he served his disciples, the "other," and his enemies. All were and are still invited to the table to receive the bread and the cup, his body and blood, his presence and life. Today, we are called to live out this hospitality through how we share our lives and with whom we share them. To follow Jesus' example, we must find ways to serve the "other" and the enemy and provide a place for everyone at our tables.

BENEDICTION

Now, may the God who came to serve remind you this day how it looks to do likewise. May the one who came and took on the position of the lowest in the house remind you that the kingdom comes humbly. May you follow the example of the king whose hands hold a towel rather than a sword.

What are some of the best meals you can remember? What made them so special?

If you could invite anyone to dinner, who would it be and why? If you could be invited by anyone to dinner, who would invite you and why?

When are you most likely to extend hospitality to someone? When are you least likely to extend hospitality to someone?

What groups in your church do you think are furthest from one another relationally?

Where do you think God's shalom can be seen today?

What did you think about the response of the LDS to the makers of *South Park* and *The Book of Mormon*? What would your response have been?

Discuss some of the projects you worked on in this chapter. How did God transform you through them? How did they help you better understand the story, yourself, others, and the world around you?

Small Group

TRANSFORMATION QUESTIONS

Chapter Nine

CONTINUING THE STORY

THE NEVERENDING STORY

In a pivotal scene near the beginning of the 1984 epic fantasy film *The NeverEnding Story*, the main character, Bastian Bux (played by Barret Oliver), ducks into a bookstore to avoid some bullies. While hiding inside, he has what will be a life-changing conversation with the grumpy bookstore owner, Mr. Coreander (played by Thomas Hill). Let's pick up the conversation midstream:

> **Mr. Coreander**: Your books are safe. While you're reading them, you get to become Tarzan or Robinson Crusoe.
>
> **Bastian**: But that's what I like about 'em.
>
> **Mr. Coreander**: Ah, but afterwards you get to be a little boy again.
>
> **Bastian**: What do you mean?
>
> **Mr. Coreander**: Listen. Have you ever been Captain Nemo, trapped inside your submarine while the giant squid is attacking you?
>
> **Bastian**: Yes.
>
> **Mr. Coreander**: Weren't you afraid you couldn't escape?
>
> **Bastian**: But it's only a story.
>
> **Mr. Coreander**: That's what I'm talking about. The ones you read are safe.
>
> **Bastian**: And that one isn't?[1]

The book Bastian receives from Mr. Coreander is the *NeverEnding Story* and it is *not* safe! Bastian enters into a fantasy world, complete with a princess, a warrior, and, of course, a villain. Yet what makes this book unsafe for Bastian is not the story itself as much as the demand it places on him to participate. Bastian realizes he can't simply read this book and walk away. The story forces him to take action—and it changes who he is from that day forward.

Many of us approach the Bible like Bastian reads his stories at the beginning of the movie. There are points throughout that captivate us, points that bore us, and even some points that frighten or alarm us. We can pick it up and put it down as we choose, and compartmentalize it to being "only a story" that never really affects how we live. For example, the parable of the Good Samaritan has all the elements of a good story. We read it and get sucked into the story, but moments later we walk away, forgetting everything God was trying to use the story to say and do in and through us. We put the book down and remain unchanged, and our world is robbed of the change God has called us to be.

So how can we begin to move past viewing the Bible as a "safe" book? How can we begin to see the Bible as real, exciting, and dangerous, as a story that forces us to be transformed or get left behind? We must start by picking up our Bible, dusting it off, and *reading* it. After all, the stories can't change us if we don't know them. We're not talking about some religious duty or about reading for a few moments, saying a prayer, and checking off our devotions for the day. Our devotion needs to be in rolling up our sleeves and diving into the dialogue that God has called us to join him in, and this dialogue can't take place alone. The community of Christ is called to read and wrestle with the story together!

It won't be easy. Dangerous stories never are. They will challenge us to find ourselves in his grand story and to, therefore, live inside a new reality—a reality in which anything is possible. And the possibilities are not based on our faith but on his character. Maybe this is why living dangerously is so scary for us—because it takes the control out of our hands! As we give up control, we willingly surrender our wants and desires for those of the kingdom.

How has the story of the Good Samaritan challenged you? How has it changed you?

React to this quote: "We put the book down and remain unchanged, and our world is robbed of the change God has called us to be."

How can we read the Bible more dangerously?

Who do you read the story with? How do you challenge each other?

Questions

Project

WRESTLING WITH THE WORD

Pick a difficult passage of scripture and wrestle with it. If you can't think of an example, try one of these: 1 Samuel 15; Job 1:6-22; Psalm 58; Ezekiel 33:1-20; Hosea 3:1-5; Luke 14:25-35; or 2 Corinthians 6:14-7:1. You probably won't like what you read. You will be forced to ask hard questions of the text, and the text will probably ask hard questions of you. We would also suggest reading surrounding passages in order to understand the passage in its larger context. You may need to bring others into the conversation to help work through the passage and to understand it as part of the grander story and as part of our own stories.

Go and Do Likewise

"Go and do likewise." These are the last four words of our passage, and they are powerful. Jesus' words to "go and do" force us to action. They are not optional for those who follow him. Let's take a moment to examine each of these words in a bit more depth.

- **Go**—This command requires movement. It requires us to leave what is comfortable and move toward what is unknown. It requires us to let go of the reins and allow God to reign. It requires us to trust, not only God, but who we are in God. It requires vulnerability and accountability.

- **And**—This word connects. It connects movement to action and, thus, assures that we will not move aimlessly. It gives hope of a destination, or several destinations, on the journey. It connects us to God and to others.

- **Do**—This command requires action. It requires sacrifice and sweat. It requires love (because "doing" without love is just a clamoring cymbal). It requires us to stop moving for a moment in order that we may see the unseen in hopes that there will be a time when the unseen are seen. And, it too requires vulnerability and accountability.

- **Likewise**—This word emulates. It tells us that we must watch and learn how Christ went and did so we can go and do likewise. It also means that we must look to others for examples and that others will look to us as examples. It means that there is a pattern for love, a pattern for Christ-likeness, and this pattern is found in "going" and "doing" out of our very "being"—being like him.

Like the Samaritan, we go and do because we know that our actions are a direct result of where we have seen Christ go and what we have seen him do. Our actions are a result of who we are in Christ, which means that we are to be intentional about finding ways to serve and loving people in our sphere of influence. It also means we are called to always be extending this sphere of influence to include the "other" and even the enemy. But, even more than these, it means that we must learn to hear the still, small voice of God speaking to our hearts and minds in the midst of the chaos of our everyday lives.

The true fruit of a life transformed by Christ is an ability to see and serve the other in the moments when no one is watching. It is in these "ordinary" moments that our lives become extraordinary. It is here that we live out of his resources rather than our own. As we do so, we not only survive but thrive, and we become what we were created to be.

These words—"go and do likewise"—remind us of some other words spoken by Jesus. In what we refer to as the Great Commission, Jesus says:

> "Therefore go and make disciples of all nations, baptizing them in the name of the Father and of the Son and of the Holy Spirit, and teaching them to obey everything I have commanded you. And surely I am with you always, to the very end of the age." (Matthew 28:19-20)

In reading these words, it is obvious that Jesus intended his disciples to continue the work he began. And just as he instructed those who came directly after him, he also commands us to "go and do likewise." But what should living out this command look like? In the past 2,000 years, the Great Commission has been used to justify a number of evangelistic endeavors—some good, but others terribly misguided. While we certainly aren't opposed to evangelism, we are instructed to *make disciples*, which requires us to invest our lives into other people rather than sharing the Gospel with them and leaving them to figure out its implications on their own.

This truth speaks volumes into our passage on the Good Samaritan. Emulating the actions of the Samaritan will cost us more than a passing word, a well-intended prayer, or a one-time service project. It will cost us our whole lives. Look again at the Samaritan's actions:

1. He was flexible with his time. He saw a need and was willing to stop what he was doing to help the person in need. In other words, it was inconvenient.

2. He was generous with his resources. Everything he had was available to the man in need: his clothes (it is likely that he tore off a piece of his garment to make bandages), his wine, his oil, his donkey, and his money. In other words, it wasn't free.

3. He was sacrificial with his life. He put the safety of the man ahead of his own safety, being willing to risk disease or death to care for this wounded man. In other words, he wasn't safe.

While this parable doesn't tell us the end of the story, we suspect that when the Samaritan returned to check on the wounded man, the man would have been not only grateful, but curious about why the Samaritan helped him. A door would have been opened for the relationship to move toward discipleship.

So what are we trying to say here?

We must look for opportunities to make disciples. We truly believe that Christ is "'the way and the truth and the life'" (John 14:6): for this reason, we must be eager and devoted to helping others enter into the same life-transforming (and we believe *world*-transforming) relationship we have entered into. Yet, we must learn what it means to love unconditionally and sacrificially even if the others we serve have no interest in Christ and never come into a relationship with him.

Questions

What prevents you from "going and doing likewise?" Don't answer too generally. Think of a particular situation when you knew you should have done something and you didn't. Why didn't you?

How do you make time in your life to hear God's still, small voice? When do you hear him most clearly? What would it take to start being able to hear him in the midst of the chaos of your everyday life?

Define discipleship. How have you been discipled? How have you discipled others? If you haven't, what prevents you from doing so?

We described the Samaritan's actions as inconvenient, not free, and not safe; which of these concerns you the most as you try to love the other? Why?

THE SAMARITAN WAY

Think of a few people whom you believe live out the characteristics of the Samaritan in our parable. How are they flexible with their time? How are they generous with their resources? How are they sacrificial with their life? Now take time today to embody one of these three characteristics.

1. **Do something inconvenient.**

   Be flexible with a moment of your time today. Spend that time serving a coworker, a fellow student, an acquaintance, or someone else who might cross your path.

2. **Do something generous.**

   Be willing to give something you have to someone who may need it today. Give an item to someone in need or buy lunch for a person you find difficult to deal with.

3. **Do something risky.**

   Be adventurous; do for someone something that is outside your normal routine. Pay for a stranger's coffee or reach out to a person you have not been able to reconcile with.

Project

REVERBERATIONS OF CHRIST

Consider times when you have experienced great joy, such as your wedding day, the first day at a new job, the thrill of holding your child for the first time, or simply being surrounded by your family on Christmas Day. Once these experiences touched you to the core, once they became part of who you were, you couldn't help but share them; they poured out of you because they *were* you. They became part of the characteristics and experiences that continue to define who you are! In the same way, we have been called to allow Christ to become such an integral part of who we are that he begins to shine through everything we do, say, and even think.

When the apostle Paul said, "To live is Christ and to die is gain" (Philippians 1:21), he wasn't intending to coin a snappy Christian T-shirt slogan. He was talking about a new reality that had so radically changed him that it affected every part of his life and everyone with whom he came in contact. He was saying that his life was no longer his own; it was Christ's. Paul, the disciples, and many women and men throughout history understood a very important truth. They understood that the lives they were living were not theirs alone. They understood that as followers of Christ, they were living out and even extending the grand story. They were revealing the already-not yet kingdom to the world around them, and they were doing it intentionally!

In the same way, we too are called to let our light shine before others, that they may see our good deeds and glorify our Father in heaven (see Matthew 5:16). We live out the story so that others will see the kingdom and the king. We live out the story because it is who we are. We are salt. We are light. We are the reverberations of Christ. We are the effects of the resurrected Christ. In and through him, the Church has echoed throughout history with the truth of the gospel. We are the repetitive sound of hope, truth, love, and joy for every new generation. We are indeed among God's chosen instruments.

What have been some of the most exciting
moments of your life so far? How have
they shaped you?

Have you experienced a life-changing
encounter with God? Have you allowed
this experience to take root within you? If
so, reflect on this experience; if not, reflect
on what you think this experience might
look like.

Questions

What does it mean to reverberate with the
truth of the gospel?

Project

IMAGE BEARERS

In this section we looked at a number of metaphors for what it means to live out God's good news. Reflect back on some of our images of musical instruments, salt, light, and so on. Think of another image that you might use to describe what it means to be a present witness as a Christ follower in our world. Draw a picture of that image in your journal. How does this image describe our role to be bearers of good news to our culture? Think of some people who live out that image in our time.

WHAT NOW?

"The journey of a thousand miles begins with one step."

This old Chinese proverb credited to Confucius is more than a bit tired, but we think it's still applicable. We hope you'll forgive us if you disagree. Either way, though, take a step. Toward Christ. Toward the other. Toward your enemy. Toward love.

If you are not already part of a faith community where you actively share in God's and each other's stories, find one. If you are not already reading the "unsafe" Bible and trying to live out and extend the story, get started. If you are not already sacrificially surrendering your time, resources, and life over to others for the sake of Christ, what are you waiting for?

God has called all of us. So, let's start the conversations and explore more deeply the ones we're already having. As we learn to listen more and speak less, may we seek to be authentic and admit our faults as we journey together.

What would it take for you to get involved with a small group of people and start living out a dangerous faith?

How might you surrender your life to Christ in tangible ways today?

Questions

GO AND DO LIKEWISE

Think back through the journey of this book. Take time to think about the many actions God may have brought to mind through your reading, journaling, or discussing. Maybe it was inviting someone to a meal. Maybe it was giving someone a gift. Maybe it was calling someone you have not spoken to in a while. In the space provided below, list three things you will do in the coming week to take the next steps toward living out the parable, toward transformation, toward God. Then go and do them!

1.

2.

3.

CONCLUSION

We have journeyed far from where we began. We have moved from passive involvement in the story to the challenge to radically participate in God's grand story. We have grappled with the questions we ask and the questions Scripture is asking of us. We have focused on being real and recognizing who we are at different points along the journey. We have learned to embrace what God is trying to teach us both in the good and bad times. We have sought to define neighbor as Jesus did and broaden our understanding of those God is calling us to serve and to love. We have wrestled with the very real problem of distance, both positive and negative. We have sought to lessen the distance between ourselves and the other and to learn what it means to serve and love unconditionally in the midst of a world where this seems foreign.

So now we come to the end of yet another story. But like every good story, we hope it is just the beginning of the conversation. We hope that everyone who reads this book will seek to continue the story of the Good Samaritan in his or her own lives and own communities. We pray that love will abound in new ways to new people. Most of all, we pray that Christ will be reflected in the Church so that the world might experience hope.

BENEDICTION

Now, may the God of new beginnings and endless possibilities be reflected in your very being. May he continue to become part of who you are at your core so that others see him in you. May you surround yourself with a community of travelers who journey with you in the midst of a hurting world and bring love, peace, justice, and hope. May you live out the story faithfully and fearlessly and in so doing, may you be an extension of the story to others.

Respond to this quote: "We are the repetitive sound of hope, truth, love, and joy for every new generation. We are indeed among God's chosen instruments." Discuss a time when this statement has been true for the Church and for you and a time when it hasn't been true.

Reflect on the book as a whole. What chapters spoke to you the most? Share some of the things you are still wrestling with from the book.

What changes have you implemented in your own life as a result of reading this book or as a result of the group discussions?

Discuss some of the projects you worked on in this chapter. How did God transform you through them? How did they help you better understand the story, yourself, others, and the world around you?

What are some things that this group could start to go and do in your community? Be specific and make a plan!

Small Group

TRANSFORMATION QUESTIONS

Notes

CHAPTER 1

1. "GlobalTribe," Global Exchange, <http://www.pbs.org/kcet/globaltribe/change/btc_reality.html>.

CHAPTER 2

1. Jay M. Enoch, "History of Mirrors Dating Back 8000 Years," *Optometry and Vision Science Journal*, 83, no. 10 (2006): 775-81, <http://journals.lww.com/optvissci/Fulltext/2006/10000/History_of_Mirrors_Dating_Back_8000_Years_.17.aspx>.

2. Martin Luther King, Jr.: "I've Been to the Mountaintop" American Rhetoric: Top 100 Speeches, <www.americanrhetoric.com/speeches/mlkivebeentothemountaintop.htm>.

3. Ibid.

4. *Hotel Rwanda*. Directed by Terry George. MGM/United Artists, 2004.

CHAPTER 3

1. Jürgen Moltmann, *Theology of Hope* (Minneapolis: Fortress, 1993), 26. Translated by James W. Leitch from the German, *Theologie der Hoffnung* (Christian Kaiser Verlag, Munich, 5th ed., 1965).

2. Stanley Hauerwas and William Willimon, *Resident Aliens: Life in the Christian Colony* (Nashville: Abingdon, 1989), 77.

CHAPTER 4

1. Donald B. Kraybill, Steven M. Nolt, and David L. Weaver-Zercher, *Amish Grace: How Forgiveness Transcended Tragedy* (San Francisco: Jossey-Bass, 2007), 183.

CHAPTER 5

1. Bruce Crumley, "Behind the French Ruling on WWII Deportations of Jews," *Time*, February 18, 2009, <http://www.time.com/time/world/article/0,8599,1880118,00.html#ixzz1jpr8Fa5r>.

2. "Archives and Regional History Collections: Dr. Martin Luther King's 1963 WMU Speech Found," Western Michigan University Libraries, <http://www.wmich.edu/~ulib/archives/mlk/q-a.html>.

3. Miroslav Volf, *Exclusion and Embrace: A Theological Exploration of Identity, Otherness, and Reconciliation* (Nashville: Abingdon, 1996), 49.

4. Ibid, 40.

CHAPTER 6

1. All of these statistics and facts come from: Anup Shah, "Poverty Facts and Stats," Global Issues, last updated September 20, 2010, <http://www.globalissues.org/article/26>.

2. Shane Claiborne and Chris Haw, *Jesus for President: Politics for Ordinary Radicals* (Grand Rapids: Zondervan, 2008), 234.

3. David Kinnaman and Gabe Lyons, *UnChristian: What a New Generation Really Thinks About Christianity . . . and Why It Matters* (Grand Rapids: Baker Books, 2007), 96.

CHAPTER 8

1. Christine Pohl, *Making Room: Recovering Hospitality as a Christian Tradition* (Grand Rapids: Eerdmans, 1999), 187.

2. Ibid, 61-75.

3. Robert Smith, "On Broadway, A 'Mormon' Swipe At . . . Everything," March 24, 2011, NPR, <www.npr.org/2011/03/24/134803453/on-broadway-a-mormon-swipe-at-everything>.

4. <www.npr.org/templates/transcript/transcript.php?storyId=134803453>, no longer available as of January 4, 2012.

5. Desmond Tutu, *No Future Without Forgiveness* (New York: Doubleday, 1999), 271.

CHAPTER 9

1. *NeverEnding Story*. Directed by Wolfgang Petersen. Neue Constantin Film, 1984.